CRUSH YOUR FRESHMAN YEAR

MASTERING ACADEMICS, SOCIAL LIFE, TIME
MANAGEMENT, AND FREEDOM FOR COLLEGE
SUCCESS

JENICA ALVAREZ

TABLE OF CONTENTS

INTRODUCTION

Welcome to what might just be the most exhilarating, nerve-wracking, and transformative adventure of your life—your freshman year of college. If your emotions are swirling with anticipation and anxiety, rest assured, you're in good company. This combination of anticipation and disbelief is common among all new freshmen.

I've been right where you are— college brochures in one hand and a long list of questions in the other. My name is Dr. Jenica Alvarez, and I've spent years helping students like you not just survive, but thrive during their college years. While my primary role as a full-time professor involves teaching on the intricacies of the human body, another aspect of my job that brings me great joy is my role as an academic advisor and mentor to college students. From guiding freshmen on their first day to supporting confident seniors as they stride into final exams, my journey has encompassed every step of the college experience. My mission? To arm you with not just hope, but also give you the skills to navigate your way through college.

Drawing on over a decade of experience, I have had the honor of assisting numerous college students over the crucial first year and beyond. My roles have not only allowed me to witness the common challenges and triumphs that students face, but also to develop a deep understanding of the strategies that best support their success. This book is designed to serve as a compass for navigating college life, offering practical advice and insights that are grounded in real student experiences. Through this guide, I aim to equip freshmen with the tools they need to thrive both academically and personally in their new environment. This book is a survival kit, a secret handbook, a compilation of tried and tested strategies that have helped real students face real challenges.

In this book, you'll find more than just academic advice. Yes, we'll cover strategies to ace your classes and manage your time like a pro, but we'll also dive into how to make meaningful connections, handle the unexpected parties and yes, even the inevitable hangovers. We'll tackle everything from choosing your major to managing your money—because college isn't just about getting good grades; it's about crafting a life you can be proud of.

Every chapter of this book is packed with practical tips, real-life scenarios, and interactive elements like quizzes and checklists. These aren't just to keep you engaged; they're there to make this journey yours. Reflect, respond, and challenge yourself with these tools. They're designed to help you carve out your own path through the chaos of freshman year.

So, whether you're a first-generation student or the latest in a long line of college-goers, whether you're brimming with confidence or bristling with questions, this book is for you. It's not just about surviving your freshman year—it's about mastering it, about turning challenges into stepping stones and uncertainty into opportunity.

Let's embark on this journey together. Welcome aboard. Your future starts here.

1

FROM HIGH SCHOOL TO COLLEGE: SETTING REALISTIC EXPECTATIONS

Remember how in high school, your day was mostly structured from the morning bell to the afternoon bus ride? College flips the script. Here, freedom isn't just another word in the dictionary—it's your new reality. You choose your classes, decide when to study, decide what to eat, and even when to roll out of bed. But here's the kicker: with great freedom comes great responsibility. Suddenly, the responsibility of meeting deadlines for term papers and group projects falls squarely on your shoulders, without the close supervision and reminders from teachers or guardians.

College classes also dive deeper than high school courses, asking you not just to understand material, but to critique and discuss it. Professors are expecting you to engage, think critically, and bring fresh ideas to the table. This isn't about regurgitating facts; it's about expanding your horizon. And yes, while this means tougher exams and more substantial projects, it also paves the way for more significant personal and intellectual growth. So, gear up to flex those brain muscles like never before!

EMOTIONAL PREPAREDNESS

It's totally normal to feel a mix of exhilaration and terror when stepping into college life. One minute you're pumped about the upcoming freedom, and the next, you're sweating about how to manage it all. This emotional whirlwind isn't just common; it's an expected part of moving into a new phase of life. Managing this means recognizing when you're feeling overwhelmed and knowing it's okay to seek help. Most colleges are stocked with resources like counseling centers and student support services—there's no medal for toughing it out alone.

Building emotional resilience early on helps you handle the ups and downs of college life. Start by setting small, manageable goals and gradually stepping out of your comfort zone. See an intro session at the student center? Go for it. Feeling homesick? Call home, then plan a movie night with someone from your dorm. It's all about finding balance and allowing yourself to grow at your own pace.

SETTING ACADEMIC GOALS

Now, about those goals. Walking into college without a game plan is like trying to bake a cake without a recipe—you need a clear idea of what you want to achieve. Begin by setting achievable academic goals that are specific and time-bound. Want a 3.5 GPA? Break it down: aim for an A in Calculus and a B in History for the semester. Attach clear actions to each goal. Maybe you'll join a study group for Calculus and visit your History professor during office hours twice a month.

Remember, the key here is not just to set goals but to revisit and adjust them as you go. Maybe that 8 AM class was a mistake—no problem! Learn what works best for you and tweak your schedule next semester. Some students prefer scheduling their classes in consecutive blocks. This strategy minimizes idle periods during the day, optimizing time management and productivity. Should you find yourself with a gap between classes, it's wise to have a strategy for utilizing this time effectively. Consider studying in the library, doing a workout at the gym, enjoying a meal, or catching up with a friend.

Crafting a new routine in college is like drawing your personal road map. Start with your class schedule, then block times for studying, meals, workouts, and yes, socializing (you need to have some fun too!). Try to keep your wake-up and sleep times consistent—even on weekends. Trust me, your brain will thank you during those early morning exams.

Pro tip? Balance doesn't mean cramming every minute with activity. Build in downtime. College is a marathon, not a sprint, and you'll need those quiet moments for a mental recharge. Whether it's yoga, video games, hiking, or journaling, find what helps you reset and make it a part of your daily routine. It's not just about sticking to a schedule; it's about creating a rhythm that fits your life and your goals.

2

PREPARING FOR COLLEGE-THE SUMMER BEFORE

E mbarking on your freshman year of college marks a monumental transition—a leap from the familiar corridors of high school to the expansive, exciting halls of higher education. To ensure a smooth transition, the summer before college should be a period of preparation and planning. This chapter will guide you through the essential steps to take during these crucial months, helping you set the stage for a successful and enjoyable college experience.

ORIENTATION

Orientation is your first real taste of college life and a pivotal event that shouldn't be missed. Numerous colleges offer summer orientations over a 1-3 day period packed with tours, info sessions, and a whole lot of walking. Wear comfortable shoes and an approachable smile. Dive into every activity — and yes, that includes the cheesy icebreakers.

You will have the opportunity to meet fellow students, professors, and staff. This is a time to familiarize yourself with the campus culture, understand important academic policies, and start creating connections that will support you throughout your college journey.

Sure, orientation might seem a tad overwhelming with all the faces and information thrown your way, but trust me, it's worth it. This is your chance to absorb everything from where to find the best coffee on campus to understanding how the library system can become your new best friend during finals week.

Pro tips for making the most of orientation:

- **Engage**: Participate in sessions and workshops. These are designed not just to inform you about the college but also to ease your anxieties and answer your queries.
- **Ask questions**: Whether it's about academic programs, extracurricular activities, or campus services, no question is too trivial. This is your chance to gather as much information as possible.
- **Make connections**: Reach out to your peers and start building your network. These early friendships can be your support system far beyond freshman year.

SCHEDULE PLANNING WITH AN ACADEMIC ADVISOR

One of the most critical steps in your college preparation is setting up your class schedule with the help of an academic advisor. This interaction can set the tone for your academic journey. Your academic advisor can help you balance your course load by considering your academic and career goals. While it's important to challenge yourself, maintaining a manageable schedule is equally vital to your success.

Familiarize yourself with the core curriculum (courses all students have to take and pass like math, science, literature, etc.) requirements and the prerequisites for your intended major. This knowledge will help you make informed decisions about which courses to enroll in. Additionally, consider your future semesters by thinking ahead about the courses you might want to take. Early planning can help you avoid scheduling conflicts and missed opportunities, ensuring a smooth academic progression.

When creating your schedule, there are several key considerations to keep in mind. Firstly, if you are receiving financial aid, familiarize yourself with the course load requirements and GPA necessary to maintain your eligibility. If you have taken AP or dual-enrollment classes in high school, consult with the Registrar's office to ensure you are credited appropriately. Additionally, if you are balancing part-time or full-time employment, collaborate with your academic advisor to develop a class schedule that accommodates your work commitments. Importantly, aim to start your freshman year on a strong note. I have observed many students who indulge excessively in their initial college experiences, leading to a significant drop in their academic performance. Such students often end up exerting extra effort over subsequent years to improve their GPAs.

SCHOOL SUPPLIES

Equipping yourself with the right supplies can help alleviate some of the stress of entering a new academic environment.

Here is a list of common academic supplies that a college student might need:

1. **Laptop or Tablet** - Essential for taking notes, completing assignments, and accessing online resources.
2. **Notebook paper** - For taking notes in classes where electronic devices are not ideal.
3. **Pens and Pencils** - A variety of pens for taking notes and pencils for exams requiring them.
4. **Highlighters** - Useful for marking important information in textbooks and notes.
5. **Binder or Folders** - To organize lecture notes, assignments, and handouts. (Pro Tip: have a separate binder for each class to keep up with all class notes and assignments.)
6. **Planner or Organizer** - To keep track of assignments, exams, and meetings. (VERY IMPORTANT!)
7. **Textbooks** - Your college bookstore will know if a textbook is required for each course you are enrolled in. Some professors require an actual textbook, while others allow a digital form of the textbook. Always check for used textbooks or if you can rent a textbooks to save money. (Pro Tip: A way to recoup some of your textbook expenses is by selling them

back to the college bookstore at the end of the semester, albeit at a lower rate.)

8. **Calculator** - Necessary for courses in mathematics, sciences, and some business courses.
9. **Sticky Notes** - Helpful for quick reminders and bookmarks.
10. **Index Cards** - Useful for flashcards to aid in studying and memorization.
11. **USB Flash Drive** - For backing up important documents and easy transfer between devices.
12. **Earphones or Headphones** - For listening to lectures, music, or blocking out noise while studying.
13. **Desk Lamp** - To ensure adequate lighting for studying without straining the eyes.
14. **Paper Clips and Staples** - For organizing papers and assignments.
15. **Scissors and Tape** - Occasionally needed for projects or fixing torn study materials.

PREPARING FOR DORM LIFE

First things first, let's sort out what you absolutely need from the extras. Essentials are your survival kit—think bedding, towels, toiletries, a laptop, chargers, and maybe a mini-fridge for those midnight snack raids. These are non-negotiables. Then come the non-essentials. Fairy lights? A fancy rug? That over-sized poster of a sunset? Nice to have, but they won't make or break your college experience. Be selective, space is a luxury. Before you pack that adorable but bulky lava lamp, ask yourself, "Will this item ease my daily grind or is it just going to take up valuable desk space?" Remember, in a space as tight as a dorm room, less is often more.

Before you both show up with a microwave, have a chat with your roommate about who's bringing what. This can be a great ice-breaker! Discuss everything from appliances to cleaning supplies. You might find out that your roommate has a killer speaker system they're willing to share, saving you the trouble and space of bringing your own. This pre-arrival negotiation can help set the stage for a harmonious dorm life, preventing the infamous 'two microwaves in a 20-square-foot space' scenario.

Speaking of space, let's talk about making the most of it. Vertical storage is your best friend in a cramped dorm room. Think hanging organizers, shelves, and hooks—anything that keeps things off the floor is a win. Pro tip? Make full use of the space under your bed. Use under-bed storage containers to stow away out-of-season clothes, extra supplies, or that bulky suitcase. Just make sure to keep it neat; nothing kills the vibe of a room like a mysterious hand emerging from a clutter of chaos under your bed.

Here's a comprehensive list of common items needed for a college dorm room, ensuring both comfort and functionality:

1. **Bedding**:

- Twin XL sheets (most common dorm bed size)
- Comforter and blanket
- Pillow and pillowcases
- Mattress pad (for extra comfort)

PREPARING FOR COLLEGE-THE SUMMER BEFORE | 21

2. Bath Essentials:

- Towels (bath towels, hand towels, washcloths)
- Shower caddy
- Flip-flops (for shower use)
- Bathrobe

3. Laundry Supplies:

- Laundry basket or hamper
- Detergent
- Dryer sheets
- Stain remover
- Quarters for laundry machines (if applicable)

4. Storage Solutions:

- Under-bed storage bins
- Closet organizers (hanging shelves, shoe racks)
- Over-the-door hooks
- Drawer organizers

5. Furniture:

- Desk lamp
- Comfortable study chair (if not provided)
- Bookshelf or storage units (if space allows)
- Full-length mirror

6. Technology:

- Laptop and charger
- Power strips and extension cords
- Headphones or earbuds
- Printer (if preferred over campus printing services)

7. Kitchen Gear:

- Mini fridge (if allowed)
- Microwave (if allowed)
- Reusable water bottle
- Dishes and utensils (plate, bowl, cup, cutlery)
- Dish soap and sponge

8. Decor and Comfort Items:

- Posters and wall art (use removable adhesive strips)
- Area rug
- Throw pillows
- Curtains (if privacy is needed and allowed)

9. Personal Items and Electronics:

- Alarm clock
- Fan or space heater (check dorm regulations)
- Health and personal care items (medications, first aid kit)
- Entertainment options (books, games, streaming device)

10. **Safety, Maintenance, and Miscellaneous**:

- Flashlight
- Batteries
- Basic tool kit
- Umbrella or rain jacket
- Duct tape (for quick fixes)

PERSONALIZING YOUR SPACE

Making your dorm room feel like home is about striking a balance between personality and practicality. Within the college's guidelines, add touches that reflect your style and make you smile. A comfortable throw, a few cherished photos, or a small plant can add life to your space without overwhelming it. These personal touches can make all the difference on days when the college grind feels a bit too much, turning your dorm into a sanctuary where you can recharge and relax.

Remember, your dorm is more than just a place to sleep; it's your command center, your kitchen, your study, and your personal chill zone—it's where you'll laugh, cry, and maybe even binge-watch a little too much Netflix. Make it yours, make it practical, and above all, make it a space where you can thrive both academically and personally. Now, armed with this knowledge, go forth and transform that dorm room into a haven of efficiency and comfort!

The summer before college is a vibrant period of anticipation and preparation. By attending orientation, scheduling your classes wisely, gathering your supplies, and setting up your living space, you are getting yourself ready to be successful in college. Each of these steps is not just about preparation, but also about starting to think and act like a college student—embracing responsibility, cultivating curiosity, and building community. As you gear up for this exciting new chapter, remember that preparation is the key to confidence and success in your freshman year and beyond.

3

THE FIRST WEEK: A DAY-BY-DAY SURVIVAL GUIDE

A h, the first week of college. It's like the pilot episode of your favorite series—you get to meet all the characters and set the scene for the epic saga ahead. Let's break it down day by day, so you can script your debut week like a pro.

DAY 1: MOVE-IN DAY

Your dorm room or apartment isn't just a sleep station—it's your command center, study space, and personal sanctuary all rolled into one. Setting up this space to be functional and comfy is crucial. You should have purchased the necessities prior to move-in day: bedding, toiletries, and, of course, a good laundry hamper. Make it feel like home. A few posters, some cozy pillows, perhaps a plant or two (yes, even those notoriously hard-to-kill succulents count). These touches can transform a bland box into a cozy nook that feels welcoming after a long day of lectures. And hey, setting up a welcoming space isn't just about decor—invite your dorm neighbors over to hang out. It's the quickest hack to start building your new college community from day one.

Be prepared for a few trips to the store to pick-up items you forgot or you determine are needed to make your room feel like home. Then, think about your study area. A comfortable chair? Check. Adequate lighting? Double-check. Organized desk with all your tech in easy reach? Triple check.

DAY 2: CLASS PREPARATIONS

By Day 2, it's time to shift gears to academic mode. Start by organizing your class materials. Binders, notebooks, pens—make sure each class has its own set, so you're not mixing up your math and world history notes. Then, hit the syllabi hard. These are your road maps for each course, outlining not just when assignments are due but also giving you a heads-up on the professor's expectations and the semester's big projects.

Mark important dates on your calendar—both digital and physical. It's like setting mini-milestones for yourself. And if you're feeling particularly proactive, start sketching out a weekly schedule that allocates time for readings, homework, and review sessions. It might seem a bit much in week one, but having this framework can ease a lot of academic anxiety when things ramp up.

Navigating your way to class is a crucial part of college life. Start by familiarizing yourself with a campus map to pinpoint where each of your classes will be held. Consider how you'll get to each class. If they're within walking distance, that's great! For farther distances, check if your college offers shuttle or bus services and note the nearest stops and schedules. Biking is another popular option for students, offering both convenience and speed. If driving is your preferred mode, plan to leave early—parking can be a challenge, and arriving late to class is a common pitfall for many new students. Allot extra time during the initial days to scout out the best parking spots, ensuring a smooth and timely arrival to your classes.

Pro tip: when reviewing your syllabi, pay attention to attendance requirements, as they differ by professor. Some professors take attendance, while others may not. Also, look closely at how the professor grades. You will find professors that have only 2-3 exams for the entire semester, and others that have quizzes, exams, and projects. Last pro tip: the textbook requirements will also be listed on the syllabus. See what textbook you need to purchase or if there are additional requirements such as a lab coat, goggles, or a specific calculator.

DAY 3-5: SOCIAL AND ACADEMIC INTEGRATION

The rest of the week is a juggling act between social invitations and academic obligations. Remember, everyone is as new to this as you are and probably just as eager to make friends. So, say yes to social outings but remember to balance it with your coursework. Found a cool club that aligns with your interests? Great! Sign up and attend the first meeting.

When it comes to classes, don't just sit in the back row and scroll through your phone. Engage, ask questions, and participate. Professors notice these things, and establishing a good rapport could be beneficial down the line—think letters of recommendation, research opportunities, or even just some handy exam tips.

Also, start forming study groups. Connecting with classmates over course material is a two-for-one deal; it helps solidify your understanding of the material and broadens your social circle. Wrap up your week by reviewing what worked and what didn't. Maybe you over committed socially or underestimated the time needed for study. That's okay. Early tweaks to your routine can set a sustainable pace for the rest of the semester. Remember, college is not just about surviving, it's about thriving.

So take a deep breath, give yourself a pat on the back, and get ready to make this place your own.

4

BUILDING YOUR NEW SUPPORT SYSTEM

A lright, let's talk about your college support network. Think of it as building an athletic team—each member brings something unique to the table, from academic allies to social sidekicks. But, before you start assembling your players, there's a group of VIPs you'll want to get on your radar: your professors. Yes, those folks standing at the front of the lecture hall, armed with PowerPoint slides and the occasional bad pun, are more than just grade dispensers. They're gateways to knowledge, opportunities, and, if you play your cards right, some pretty influential connections.

HOW TO CONNECT WITH FACULTY AND WHY IT MATTERS

So, you're sitting there in a huge lecture hall, and there's this professor droning on about the existential implications of Shakespearean tragedy or the thrilling world of quantum mechanics. How do you even begin to break the ice? Here's the scoop: start by showing genuine interest. Ask questions during class (yes, even those "this might be a dumb question" questions), share your thoughts, or offer an answer. Trust me, most professors appreciate curious minds.

And here's a little secret: professors are people too (shocking, right?). They appreciate a friendly hello before or after class, a quick comment about something interesting from the lecture, or even a discussion about a related article you read. It's all about making yourself known, not just as another face in the crowd but as someone who's genuinely engaged. Think of it as planting the seeds for a blossoming academic relationship.

OFFICE HOURS AND COMMUNICATION

Now, let's talk office hours. Office hours are determined by each professor and these are times you can expect to find a professor in their office. This is your golden opportunity to receive academic insights and personalized advice. Yet, so many students do not take advantage of the weekly office hours. Here's why you shouldn't: visiting during office hours shows you're proactive and dedicated to your academic growth. It's your chance to ask detailed questions about the syllabus, discuss concepts that zigzagged over your head during lectures, or seek guidance on assignments.

When you do drop by, come prepared. Bring specific questions or topics to discuss. Not only does this make the best use of the time, but it also shows the professor you're serious about your learning. Plus, it's a quieter, more relaxed setting to build rapport and get to know your professor beyond the lecture hall.

Pro tip? A few days before you plan to visit, send a brief email to your professor to inquire about dropping by during office hours to ask some questions. This notice helps ensure the professor is prepared for your visit and can associate your name with your face more easily.

Major insider tip? When you send a professor an e-mail, make sure it is properly addressed- Dr., Mr., Mrs., or Professor. Never use their first name. Use correct grammar, spelling, and capitalization. State who you are and what course you are taking with them, keep it brief, and sign your name. Do not email them something that is formatted like a text message.

Just for laughs, here are a few emails I have received over the years from students. These are examples of what NOT to do.

"Hi, I am in group 1 and I am unable to view the video. Thanks."

"I tried to register for a class, however it would not allow me to because of a campus restriction. Thx."

"hey, i was wondering on how i find out my progress, how do i know how long I have left till i graduate?"

Personally, I have a statement in my syllabi regarding how to format an email appropriately. Here is what my syllabi state regarding appropriate communication:

"NOTE: I kindly request that you use proper etiquette in emails. Proper etiquette includes politeness, professionalism, and correct English. Do not write me an email that is written like a "text" with no punctuation or sentence structure, no greeting or signature, etc. Emails that are written in this manner may not receive a response."

BUILDING MENTOR RELATIONSHIPS

As the weeks roll by and you've broken the ice and aced the office hour visits, consider how a professor might help steer your academic and career trajectory as a mentor. Good mentors can offer invaluable guidance, from navigating your current studies to making decisions about grad school or career paths. They can provide you with realistic advice, insider knowledge, and encouragement based on their own experiences and expertise.

Start by expressing your interest in deeper learning opportunities, such as research projects or special assignments. Show initiative by asking about their career path or current research interests. Remember, a mentoring relationship is a two-way street; it requires trust, respect, and communication from both sides.

Building a solid network with faculty can open doors to recommendations, internships, and even job opportunities. Professors often have a vast network and can connect you with colleagues, industry contacts, and alumni who can offer career insights or job leads.

Engage in departmental events, guest lectures, and seminars. These are learning opportunities and networking goldmines. Be proactive, ask insightful questions, and follow up with an email thanking the speaker for their insights. It shows appreciation and keeps you on their radar. Remember, every interaction has the potential to add a brick to your career pathway, so make each one count.

CLUBS AND ORGANIZATIONS THAT MATCH YOUR INTERESTS

Stepping onto campus opens up a world of opportunities with each club and organization offering its own unique vibe and appeal. It's your chance to explore various interests, meet a wide range of people, and truly find where you belong. Whether you are deeply involved in gaming, eager to start your own business, or passionate about environmental activism, you are likely to find a group of like-minded enthusiasts eager to welcome you.

Diving into campus organizations isn't just about filling out your weekly planner with events; it's about aligning these experiences with your interests or career ambitions. Start by attending the club fair—yes, that carnival of tables loaded with sign-up sheets and candy bowls. Don't just breeze through though—chat with the members, ask about what they do, how they do it, and what they love about their group. It's like speed dating, but instead of awkward silences, you get insights into whether this could be your new squad. If public interactions aren't your jam, no stress—most clubs have social media pages or websites where you can get the lowdown on their activities and mission.

Now, why should you even bother? Picture this: you're part of a team that organizes community clean-ups, debates, or startup pitches. This involvement does more than just spruce up your resume; it deepens your college experience. You're not just attending college; you're actively shaping your environment. These experiences carve out a sense of belonging, tethering you to a community that shares your passions and values. Moreover, stepping into a leadership role, even one as seemingly minor as managing a club's Instagram account, hones skills that are gold dust in the professional world— think communication, teamwork, and problem-solving.

But here's the tricky part—keeping the balance. Juggling academics and club commitments can feel like trying to keep plates spinning on poles. Here's a strategy: prioritize. Not every club requires an all-in commitment. Maybe you decide to take a major role in one club while being a general member in a couple of others. Use tools like digital calendars to block out time for club activities around your class schedule and study time. Remember, the goal is to enrich your college life, not overwhelm it.

Expanding your social circle through these clubs can be a game-changer. Clubs aren't just about shared interests; they're about shared experiences. You'll find yourself studying for midterms together, volunteering at events, and maybe even traveling to conferences. These aren't just club mates; they become your college family, your support network, the ones you high-five at graduation and stay in touch with long after. Plus, these connections often lead to study groups that can be crucial during exams. It's like building a small community within the wider university—a community that can support you academically and socially.

In weaving these threads together—exploring interests, building communities, taking on responsibilities, and expanding networks—you're not just attending college. You're actively engaging in a vibrant, dynamic community that enhances your personal and professional growth. This active involvement sets the stage for a fulfilling college experience, ensuring you gain more than just academic knowledge but also a rich tapestry of relationships and experiences that will inform and inspire your journey long after you've tossed your graduation cap into the air. So go on, find your tribe, and start making those connections that will define your college days and beyond.

5

MASTERING TIME MANAGEMENT

Time management—often the greatest challenge faced by students. If you've ever found yourself panic-studying at 2 AM for a test you forgot about, or frantically writing a paper an hour before it's due, you're not alone. Managing your time in college can seem challenging at first, but with determination, it becomes manageable. But fear not! This chapter is all about learning how to manage your time, so you can juggle your studies, social life, and get a healthy amount of sleep.

CREATING A WEEKLY SCHEDULE THAT WORKS

First things first, let's talk about time wasters. We all have them. Maybe it's scrolling through social media, binge-watching the latest series, or figuring out which meme best describes your day. While these activities are fine in moderation, they become time wasters when they take away from the time you planned to spend on studying or sleeping. The trick is recognizing your time wasters early. Keep a log for a week: jot down everything you do and how long you spend on each activity. You'll quickly spot patterns where time seems to disappear. Once you identify these, you can start making changes, like setting a timer for social media use or swapping TV time for a study session with friends. It's about making your habits work for you, not against you.

Remember when you thought you'd never forget anything ever? Yeah, college will change that. This is where planners and apps come in handy. Whether you're old-school and prefer a physical planner or are tech-savvy and like an app, these tools are lifesavers. Apps like Google Calendar or Trello let you color-code different activities, set reminders, and even share your schedule with others (hello, group projects). They keep you on track and make sure you never miss a beat—or a deadline. Plus, there's something incredibly satisfying about swiping off a completed task. It's like telling your day, "Yeah, I owned you."

When creating a balanced schedule, start with the non-negotiables: classes and study time. Next, add in extracurriculars and social activities—these are important but adjustable. Don't forget to toss in some downtime and "you" time as it is essential to keep you happy. Aim for a mix that keeps you engaged from morning till night, but without over stuffing yourself. It might take a few tries to get it right, but once you do, you'll find that things start to flow smoother, leaving you feeling less like you're drowning in commitments and more like you're surfing on top of them.

Here's the thing about schedules—they change. An assignment might take longer than expected, or a friend might need a pep talk right when you planned to study. Flexibility is key. While it's important to stick to your schedule, it's just as important to know when to adapt. Allow some wiggle room when you plan your week. That way, when the unexpected comes, and it will, you can handle it without the rest of your plans crashing down. And remember, it's okay to reshuffle things around. The goal of your schedule is to make your life easier, not chain you to a planner.

THE IMPORTANCE OF SELF-CARE

In the whirlwind of assignments and the lively buzz of social gatherings, it's crucial not to overlook a key aspect of your college experience: your well-being. Self-care as an essential part in your college journey, one that ensures your social life and energy levels remain vibrant and balanced. Achieving enough sleep, maintaining a nutritious diet, staying active, and taking necessary mental pauses are foundational to this. Neglecting these aspects can dampen the college experience, leading to burnout and increased stress.

Make self-care a non-negotiable part of your routine. Schedule it like you would an important class. Maybe it's a yoga session between lectures or a short walk after a study marathon. These little self-care snippets can boost your energy and focus, making you more effective both socially and academically.

INTERACTIVE ELEMENT: WEEKLY PLANNING EXERCISE

To really get a grip on your new scheduling skills, why not put them into practice with a weekly planning exercise?

Here's a simple step-by-step guide to creating an effective weekly schedule:

1. **List all your weekly commitments**: Classes, work shifts, meetings, planned outings, etc.
2. **Estimate how much time each activity will take**, including travel time.
3. **Prioritize your tasks**: Mark them as high, medium, or low priority.
4. **Fill in your high-priority tasks in your planner first**, then fit the medium and low-priority ones around them.
5. **Review and adjust as necessary** at the end of each week. What worked? What didn't? Fine-tune for next week.

Grab a planner or open a new calendar app, and start blocking out your time for next week, keeping in mind everything you've just learned. By the end of this exercise, you'll not only have a clearer picture of your week but also a solid plan to tackle it head-on.

PRIORITIZATION AND DEADLINES: STAYING ON TOP WITHOUT FALLING BEHIND

Let's discuss the juggling act you're performing every day. You have assignments, social events, personal downtime, and maybe even a job. Keeping all these balls in the air without letting one drop can feel like being a circus performer. But don't worry, I have some strategies to help you keep juggling.

First up, setting priorities. Evaluate your tasks based on importance and urgency. An assignment due tomorrow? High priority. A party next week? Lower priority. Use tools like the Eisenhower Box, which divides tasks into four categories: urgent and important, important but not urgent, urgent but not important, and neither urgent nor important. This method helps you focus on what really needs your attention now and schedule the rest for later.

Now, let's tackle projects that take a while and have a hard deadline. Start by outlining the project and identifying all the steps you need to take to complete it. Then, set a deadline for each step. This approach makes the task seem less daunting and keeps you on track to finish before the final deadline. No more all-nighters before the due date! For example, if you have a term paper, set deadlines for choosing a topic, researching, writing the first draft, revising, and finalizing. Each step completed on time is a step closer to your goal.

The art of saying no is crucial too. When your plate is full, and someone asks you to take on another task, be honest. Explain that you have existing commitments and provide a realistic alternative. For instance, if a friend wants you to help plan a party, but you're swamped with studies, suggest contributing in a smaller capacity or choosing another time when your schedule is clearer. Remember, saying no isn't selfish; it's necessary to maintain your sanity and the quality of everything you do.

Procrastination, the habit of delaying tasks or decisions, often leads to unnecessary stress and reduced productivity. Procrastination often turns today's tasks into tomorrow's burdens. The key to overcoming procrastination is setting clear, achievable goals. Break your work into small, manageable tasks with specific, short-term deadlines. Create a conducive study environment, free from distractions—yes, this might mean silencing your phone for a few hours. And reward yourself for completing tasks. Finished a challenging assignment? Treat yourself to an episode of your favorite show or a coffee break. These little rewards boost your morale and reinforce your productive behavior.

Combining these strategies—prioritizing tasks, managing deadlines, saying no, and handling procrastination—turns you into a time management pro. You'll find yourself staying on top of your commitments without the last-minute stress, and you'll still have time for what's important to you, whether that's acing your courses, hanging out with friends, or just enjoying some well-earned downtime.

6

ENHANCING STUDY SKILLS

E ver had that moment when you're staring at your notes the night before an exam, and it feels like you're reading an ancient script written in a mix of hieroglyphs and alien code? Yep, we've all been there. Studying isn't just about putting in the hours; it's about making those hours count. In college, you must learn how to apply the concepts taught in class. You will not be able to simply memorize a concept and move on. Professors expect a higher level of thinking and content application. Grab your highlighters, folks—it's time to revamp how you learn and make those facts stick like superglue.

ENGAGEMENT IN THE CLASSROOM

Let's kick things off with something that might sound obvious but is often overlooked: getting involved in class. Before you dismiss this as obvious advice, take a moment to consider its impact. Active engagement in class—asking questions, participating in discussions, or even just nodding along to show you're following—can drastically boost your understanding and retention of the material.

Beyond mere class participation, minimizing distractions is equally crucial for enhancing your learning experience. This means setting aside your phone to avoid texting and scrolling, closing your laptop tabs that aren't related to class, and resisting the urge to listen to music or stream shows during lectures. Demonstrating your commitment to learning by eliminating these distractions not only benefits your academic performance but also signals to your professor your serious intent to engage with the material.

So, how do you become an engagement pro? Start small. Make a goal to ask at least one question per class or contribute one comment to the discussion. It doesn't have to be a groundbreaking observation; even curious questions or linking what the professor says to something you've read or experienced can spark a richer understanding and make the material more memorable. Plus, speaking up in class builds a rapport with your professor, and let's be honest, having them know your face and name can only help when you need that participation grade or a letter of recommendation down the line.

EFFECTIVE NOTE-TAKING METHODS

To really make your notes work for you, you need to pick a method that matches how you learn best. For some, it's classic outlining, where you structure your notes with main topics, subtopics, and details, creating a clear, hierarchical map of the lecture. For others, the Cornell method works wonders, dividing your page into cues, notes, and summary sections to help review and self-test easily.

Another popular technique is mind mapping, where you draw your notes in a web-like structure, connecting related concepts with lines or colors, making it a fantastic tool for visual learners. Experiment with different methods in different classes to see what sticks. The goal here isn't just to take notes but to create a resource that you can understand and remember when exam time rolls around.

If you are an auditory learner, ask your professor if it is okay to record the lectures. This technique allows you to fully engage in listening and understanding the material in real-time without the distraction of taking notes. Later, you can replay the recordings at your own pace, which helps reinforce the concepts discussed. This method also provides the opportunity to pause, reflect, and jot down important notes, ensuring a deeper grasp of the subject matter and more effective retention.

STUDY GROUPS

Now, let's talk about the powerhouse of learning: study groups. These aren't just for tackling tougher subjects or dividing up review topics; they're a goldmine for enhancing your understanding through explanation, debate, and shared insights. When you verbalize your thoughts and answer peers' questions, you're not just helping them—you're reinforcing your own knowledge. It's like teaching a mini-class; you learn almost as much as your listeners.

To get the most out of study groups, keep them small—three to five members is ideal. Choose people who are as committed as you are and aim to meet regularly, whether in person or via video calls. Set clear goals for each session, like reviewing a chapter or discussing a case study, and make sure everyone comes prepared. This keeps your sessions focused and productive, making them something you look forward to rather than a dreaded obligation.

INTERACTIVE LEARNING TOOLS

And because we're in the glorious age of technology, let's not forget the array of interactive tools at your disposal. From flashcards apps like Anki to quiz platforms like Quizlet, these resources make studying active, engaging, and even fun. Flashcards, for example, are perfect for memorizing definitions, dates, or formulas, and the spaced repetition algorithm that many apps use helps you focus on concepts you haven't yet mastered.

Incorporate these tools into your regular study sessions to spice things up and add variety to your learning routine. They're especially handy for quick reviews between classes or during downtime, turning idle time into productive mini-study sessions. Plus, many of these platforms allow you to create your own study materials or use sets shared by other students, giving you access to a wide range of pre-made resources.

INTERACTIVE ELEMENT: QUICK QUIZ ON LEARNING STYLES

To wrap up this section and get a better handle on which study techniques might suit you best, why not take a quick quiz on learning styles? Understanding whether you're a visual, auditory, reading/writing, or kinesthetic learner can help you tailor your study methods to fit your natural preferences. Here's a simple quiz to get you started. Choose the option that best describes your usual approach or preference.

1. When trying to remember a phone number, I:

   A) Picture the digits in my mind.
   B) Repeat it to myself out loud.
   C) Write it down or type it out.
   D) Tap out the rhythm of the numbers.

2. I understand a new concept best when I:

   A) See a graph or chart.
   B) Hear someone explain it.
   C) Read about it or see it written down.
   D) Use my hands or body to explore it.

3. When giving directions, I prefer to:

   A) Draw a map or provide pictures.
   B) Give verbal instructions.
   C) Write them down.
   D) Walk or drive the route with them.

4. I find it easier to stay focused when I am:

A) Watching a video or looking at something.
B) Listening to a lecture or discussion.
C) Reading or writing about the topic.
D) Moving around or making something.

5. When assembling something new, like furniture, I prefer to:

A) Look at the diagram.
B) Have someone tell me the steps.
C) Read the instruction manual.
D) Dive in and learn through trial and error.

6. I enjoy spending my free time:

A) Watching movies or visiting art galleries.
B) Listening to music or podcasts.
C) Reading books or writing.
D) Playing sports or engaging in hands-on activities.

7. I find I remember information better when I:

A) Visualize it as a picture or use color-coding.
B) Discuss it or listen to it being explained.
C) Rewrite my notes or organize them differently.
D) Teach it to someone else or act it out.

8. When trying to solve a problem, I:

  A) Draw it out or visualize different scenarios.
  B) Talk through the options.
  C) Write down the steps and analyze them.
  D) Build models or simulate the situation.

Scoring System:

- Tally up the number of A, B, C, and D responses.
- The category with the highest score indicates your preferred learning style:

- **Mostly A's:** Visual Learner
- **Mostly B's:** Auditory Learner
- **Mostly C's:** Reading/Writing Learner
- **Mostly D's:** Kinesthetic Learner

Here are study strategies tailored for each different type of learner:

Visual Learner

1. **Use Color Coding:** Highlight notes with different colors to categorize and remember information better.
2. **Create Mind Maps:** Visualize relationships between concepts by drawing mind maps or diagrams.
3. **Watch Videos:** Utilize educational videos and animations to grasp complex subjects.

Auditory Learner

1. **Record Lectures:** Use audio recordings of lectures to listen to them again for better retention.
2. **Participate in Discussions:** Engage in group discussions or study groups where verbal exchange of ideas can occur.
3. **Use Mnemonic Devices:** Create rhymes or songs to remember facts and figures.

Reading/Writing Learner

1. **Rewrite Notes:** Take detailed notes during class and rewrite them neatly to reinforce learning.
2. **Summarize Texts:** Write summaries of chapters or articles to condense and recall information.
3. **Read Extensively:** Engage with a wide range of texts beyond textbooks, such as scholarly articles and journals.

Kinesthetic Learner

1. **Use Physical Activities:** Integrate physical activities into studying, like walking while reviewing flashcards.
2. **Engage in Practical Experiments:** Whenever possible, apply theories in practical experiments or real-world scenarios.
3. **Create Models:** Build models or use physical objects to represent and examine abstract concepts.

These tailored approaches can help students enhance their learning efficiency by aligning with their natural preferences.

EXAM STRATEGIES THAT MAXIMIZE YOUR SCORES

Exams—the big leagues of your college experience where all your hard work gets put to the test, literally. Whether it's the multiple-choice questions that make you second-guess yourself, essay exams that have you channeling your inner Shakespeare, or open-book exams that aren't as straightforward as they seem, each type demands a unique approach to studying. Let's break down how to tailor your study strategy to fit the exam type, ensuring you're not just memorizing information, but really understanding it.

For multiple-choice exams, it's tempting to just memorize facts and figures. However, understanding the concepts behind those facts is what will save you when you're faced with tricky questions designed to catch you out on technicalities. When taking multiple choice tests, having effective strategies can significantly improve performance.

Here are some key testing strategies:

1. **Read All Options:** Before selecting an answer, carefully read each option. Sometimes, the options may contain similar answers, and only one is correct.
2. **Eliminate Wrong Answers:** Use the process of elimination to narrow down your choices. Cross out any answers you know are incorrect to clarify your

choices and increase the likelihood of picking the right one.

3. **Look for Keywords:** Pay attention to keywords in the question and answers. These can often guide you to the correct choice, especially if the language in the question is reflected in one of the answers.

4. **Understand the Question:** Make sure you fully understand what the question is asking. Sometimes, misinterpreting the question can lead you to choose the wrong answer.

5. **Use Logical Deduction:** Apply logical reasoning to deduce the correct answer, especially when you are unsure. Think about the implications of each answer choice and how they relate to what you have studied.

6. **Watch for Qualifiers:** Words like "always," "never," "all," and "none" are absolute qualifiers that can make an answer incorrect. Conversely, words like "usually," "often," "some," and "rarely" are more flexible and may often be correct.

7. **Guess Strategically:** If you must guess, do so strategically. After eliminating the clearly wrong answers, choose among the remaining options. If two options seem similar, they might be more likely to be correct.

8. **Review Your Answers:** If time allows, go back and review your answers, especially those you were unsure about. Be cautious about changing answers; often, your first instinct is correct unless you find a clear reason to change.

9. **Manage Your Time:** Keep track of time and pace yourself to ensure that you have enough time to

answer all questions. Avoid spending too much time on any single question.

10. **Practice with Sample Questions:** Familiarize yourself with the format and types of questions you can expect by practicing with sample tests. This practice can help you become more efficient and confident.

Essay exams require a different set of strategies than multiple choice tests. Here are five effective strategies for preparing for and taking essay exams:

1. **Understand the Prompt:** Before you begin writing, make sure you fully understand the question or prompt. Identify key terms and tasks, such as "compare," "contrast," "discuss," or "evaluate." This understanding will guide your response and ensure you address what is asked.

2. **Plan Your Essay:** Spend the first few minutes planning your essay. Outline your main points and examples in a brief outline to organize your thoughts and create a clear structure. This helps keep your essay focused and prevents you from veering off topic.

3. **Use a Clear Structure:** Structure your essay with a clear introduction, body, and conclusion. The introduction should set up your thesis or main argument, the body should support this with several well-organized paragraphs, and the conclusion should summarize the main points and restate the thesis in light of the evidence discussed.

4. **Incorporate Specific Examples:** Use specific examples to support your arguments. These can be from the course material, readings, or relevant research. Specific examples demonstrate your understanding of the material and strengthen your arguments.

5. **Review and Revise:** If time permits, review your essay before submitting it. Check for any grammatical errors, unclear statements, or paragraphs that could be strengthened. Make sure each paragraph flows logically to the next, and your essay as a whole supports your thesis.

Open-book exams might sound like a breeze since you can use your textbooks and notes, but they're really a test of how well you understand and can apply concepts quickly. Organize your resources beforehand with tabs and annotations, so you don't waste precious time during the exam searching for information. Focus on grasping the broader concepts and relationships between topics, as these exams often ask for more in-depth analysis.

If you're still cramming the night before an exam, let's try a different tactic. Spaced repetition is a game changer—it involves spreading out your studying over several sessions, which helps move information into your long-term memory more effectively than a last-minute marathon session. Tools like flashcards work well with this method; review them regularly, increasing intervals between sessions as you become more familiar with the material. Another powerful technique is teaching the material to someone else. Yes, grab a friend, a family member, or even your pet (they're great listeners), and explain the concepts to them. Teaching is a great way to deepen your understanding and spot any weak areas in your knowledge.

Exam anxiety is real and can throw a wrench in your performance, but managing it is totally within your reach. Start with good preparation; it's the foundation for confidence. Make sure you understand the material and have practiced under exam conditions. On the exam day, keep a few stress-relief tricks up your sleeve: deep breathing exercises, positive visualization (picture yourself acing the exam), and a quick stretching session before you start. These can help calm your nerves and sharpen your focus. Also, maintain a healthy routine leading up to exams—get plenty of sleep, eat well, and hydrate. Your brain needs fuel to perform at its best.

Lastly, don't skip the post-exam reflection. Whether you aced it or feel like you could have done better, take some time to review how you did. Look over your exam when you get it back and make note of where you excelled and where you stumbled. Discuss your answers with your professor to get clarity on any mistakes, and use this feedback to adjust your study strategies for next time. This reflection process turns every exam into a learning experience, helping you improve continuously throughout your college years.

Remember, each strategy we've discussed is a tool in your academic toolkit. Whether it's adapting your study habits to different types of exams, leveraging powerful revision techniques, managing exam stress, or learning from each experience, these strategies are designed to empower you, not just for your next test, but for any challenge college throws your way. Next up, we'll dive into making meaningful connections—because college isn't just about hitting the books; it's also about building relationships that enrich your academic journey and beyond. Get ready to expand your network and enhance your college experience in ways you never imagined!

7

MAKING MEANINGFUL CONNECTIONS

Contrary to what you may think, you're not in college to grab a degree off the shelf and bolt; you're there to mingle, meet, and maybe merge paths with folks who could impact your future in ways you've never imagined. Yes, I'm talking about networking. Networking in college is about building genuine connections that can help steer you both now and far beyond graduation. It's less about collecting contacts and more about cultivating relationships that enrich both your professional and personal growth.

First off, let's dismantle some misconceptions: networking isn't just for business majors, and it certainly isn't something you postpone until your senior year scramble. Every classmate, professor, guest speaker, or alumni event attendee could play a pivotal role in your future. By weaving a web of contacts now, you're setting up a support system, a sounding board, and yes, a launchpad for career opportunities.

So, how does this magic happen? It's all about engaging—sharing ideas in class discussions, joining clubs, showing up at guest lectures, and yes, even chatting with folks in line at the cafeteria. Each interaction has the potential to open a new door, offer a new perspective, or even lead to a job offer down the line. Remember, today's fellow student could be tomorrow's industry leader, and the relationship you build now could be the cornerstone of your future network.

BUILDING A PROFESSIONAL ONLINE PRESENCE

Now, let's talk digital footprint. In today's world, your online persona can be just as important as your real-life demeanor. Sites like LinkedIn are not just online resumes; they are platforms where you can showcase your achievements, share your academic projects, and connect with industry professionals.

Start by crafting a clear, professional LinkedIn profile. Use a decent head-shot—not that blurry photo from last year's beach party—and a headline that reflects your career aspirations. Regularly update your accomplishments, whether it's a new project you've aced, a workshop you attended, or a part-time job you've managed. Engage with content relevant to your field by sharing articles, commenting on posts, and participating in discussions. This keeps you visible and active, showing potential employers or mentors that you're engaged and informed.

ATTENDING CAMPUS EVENTS

Stepping out from behind your screen is crucial, too. Your campus is a goldmine of opportunities with guest lectures, career fairs, networking nights, and industry seminars often on offer. Mark these on your calendar and make it a point to attend. Dress smart—no, you don't need a three-piece suit, but maybe leave the ripped jeans at home—and come prepared with questions or talking points.

Here's where the magic of serendipity comes into play. You might bump into an alum who works in your dream company or a professor who's connected with industry leaders. These events are not just about listening passively; they're about participating actively. Ask questions during Q&A sessions, introduce yourself to speakers, exchange contact details, and follow up with a polite thank you email, referencing something specific from the event to jog their memory. It's these small, personal touches that can turn a brief encounter into a lasting connection.

EFFECTIVE COMMUNICATION SKILLS

Alright, so you've made some contacts. Great! But the real art lies in keeping these connections alive and kicking. Effective communication is key—be it via email, social media, or good old-fashioned face-to-face chats. When reaching out to a new contact, be concise yet friendly, professional yet personable. Express genuine interest in their work or insights and, if you're asking for advice, be specific about what you're seeking.

Maintaining these relationships requires a delicate balance. You don't want to be the person who only reaches out when you need a favor. Instead, check in occasionally with updates on your progress or interesting articles related to their field. Celebrate their achievements with a quick congratulatory note. It's about fostering a two-way street where mutual respect and interest are the foundation.

INTERACTIVE ELEMENT: NETWORKING CHALLENGE

To put your newfound networking skills to the test, here's a fun challenge: attend at least one networking event this month and connect with at least three people. After the event, follow up with a personalized email or LinkedIn message. Keep track of these new connections with a simple spreadsheet or a note on your phone, noting interesting facts or topics you discussed. This will make future conversations easier and more personal, helping you build a network that's not just wide, but also deep.

Networking isn't just a skill; it's an art. It's about weaving together a tapestry of relationships that can support, enhance, and potentially catapult your career to new heights. So step out, reach out, and connect. Your future network starts now.

Strategies for Making New Friends and Building Lasting Relationships

When you first step foot on your college campus, you might find the sea of new faces intimidating. But fear not! Making friends in college is less about having slick social skills and more about finding common ground and being your genuine self.

Initiating friendships can be as simple as connecting with others who share your passions. Whether it's a shared enthusiasm for anime, a dedication to environmental causes, or a mutual interest in mastering the art of espresso, finding common ground is key. College clubs and organizations provide a setting for these connections, offering a space where you can engage in your hobbies while forging friendships over shared interests. Whether you're into poetry, robotics, or salsa dancing, there's almost always a group of people who are into the same thing. Dive into club meetings, join group activities, and don't shy away from initiating conversations about your shared interests.

First impressions can be powerful, and often, your body language speaks before you do. Adopting an open posture, maintaining eye contact, and smiling are like the human equivalent of saying, "Hey, I'm friendly and approachable!" It's about making others feel comfortable in your presence, which in turn, makes it easier for them to strike up a conversation with you.

Staying open to new experiences plays a big role too. College is full of opportunities, and sometimes stepping out of your comfort zone by attending a new club meeting or saying yes to a study group invitation can lead to friendships that last a lifetime. Each new experience is a door to meeting new people.

Friendships deepen not just through shared interests but through shared stories and experiences. Being a good listener is crucial here. It's about more than just hearing words; it's about understanding emotions and perspectives. When someone shares something with you, show genuine interest. Ask thoughtful questions, nod to show you're following, and offer feedback that shows you truly grasp what they're saying. This kind of empathetic engagement builds trust and shows that you value the friendship beyond surface-level interactions.

In your conversations, strive to be as open about your thoughts and feelings as you want them to be about theirs. This mutual exchange fosters a deeper connection, turning casual acquaintances into lifelong friends. Remember, a conversation is a two-way street; it's about giving as much as you're receiving.

NAVIGATING FRIENDSHIPS IN A DIGITAL AGE

In the era of digital communication, maintaining friendships often extends beyond face-to-face interactions. Social media platforms can be fantastic tools for staying connected, sharing daily snippets, and coordinating meetups. However, they come with their own set of challenges. It's easy to get caught up in the number of likes or the online persona and forget about nurturing real connections.

Use social media wisely. Let it be a tool that enhances your friendships, not replaces them. Share, but also make time for offline interactions. Remember, a digital "like" is no substitute for a heart-to-heart talk, a shared meal, or a laughter-filled hangout. Be mindful of heavily relying on digital communication, especially when it comes to discussing more serious or personal matters. Some conversations are best had face-to-face, where misunderstandings that often arise from text messages can be easily avoided.

As you navigate through these strategies, remember that building friendships is a journey, not a race. It's about finding your people, connecting on a deeper level, and nurturing those relationships through shared experiences, empathy, and genuine interactions, both online and offline. So take your time, be yourself, and let the connections unfold naturally. You're not just building friendships; you're creating a community that will enrich your college experience and support you long after graduation.

8

DORM LIFE ETIQUETTE AND CONFLICT RESOLUTION

First and foremost, recognize that your dorm is a shared space. Everyone is working toward their personal goals with the collective aim of excelling academically. Maintaining a low noise level is essential. Establish clear rules around noise, particularly during the night, to respect everyone's need for quiet. Remember, noise isn't limited to just blasting music or the sound of the television; even the ring of an alarm or whispers from late-night conversations can disturb others. A practical piece of advice? Invest in high-quality headphones.

Then there's the guest policy. Sure, it's fun to have friends over, but it's not so fun for your roommate if they're stumbling over someone's backpack in the middle of the night. Always check with your roomies before inviting people over, and keep the visits reasonable. No one wants a third, unofficial roommate who's always on the couch.

Shared spaces like the bathroom and kitchen can be tricky. Piece of advice- leave them better than you found out them.

If you make a mess, clean it up. Used the last of the milk? Replace it. It's all about respecting the space and the people you share it with. A clean, organized dorm is more than just pleasant—and it's a stress reducer.

Set expectations early. Sit down with your roommates at the start of the semester and decide how you'll handle cleaning, guests, eating each other's food, and borrowing each other's stuff. It might feel a bit formal, but it's significantly better than a mid-semester meltdown over dishes or disappearing snacks. Getting these agreements in writing might seem over the top, but it's a great reference when memories get fuzzy. Plus, it shows you're all committed to making the shared space work.

RESPECTING PERSONAL SPACE AND BELONGINGS

Respecting personal space and belongings goes beyond not borrowing your roommate's clothes without asking. It's about recognizing that even in a shared space, everyone needs a little corner they can call their own. Whether it's a designated desk, a side of the room, or even a shelf, keeping your stuff to your space can be the silent glue that holds the roommate relationship together.

SHARING RESPONSIBILITIES

Sharing responsibilities doesn't mean you need to draw up a chore wheel (though, hey, if that's your jam, spin away!). It's about ensuring one person isn't left feeling like the maid. Maybe you handle vacuuming, and your roommate takes out the trash. Or you alternate weeks for cleaning the bathroom. The key here is clarity and fairness. Regular check-ins can help keep everyone accountable and resentment at bay.

PRIVACY AND ALONE TIME

Even the most extroverted people need a moment to themselves. Recognizing and respecting this need is crucial. Maybe it's as simple as using headphones while watching videos or stepping out to take calls. Discuss how you'll handle these needs and what signals (like a closed door) mean.

Imagine you've had a rough day; you're stressed, homesick, or just tired. Sometimes, you just need a bit of space to unwind without social interaction. Communicating this need respectfully ensures that when you hang that "do not disturb" sign on your door handle, your roommate knows it's your time to recharge, no hard feelings involved.

INTERACTIVE ELEMENT: ROOMMATE AGREEMENT TEMPLATE

To get you started, here's a basic template for a roommate agreement. Tailor it to meet your specific needs:

Roommate Agreement Plan

Date: [Insert Date]

Roommates: [Insert Names of All Roommates]

1. Personal Information

- **Name and Contact Info**: List each roommate's name along with preferred contact information (e.g., phone number, email).

2. Rent and Utilities

- **Rent**: [Specify the amount each roommate pays and the due date.]
- **Utilities**: [List the utilities e.g., electricity, water, internet. Specify how these bills are divided and payment arrangements.]

3. Chores and Responsibilities

- **Cleaning Duties**: [Detail each roommate's responsibilities for keeping the shared spaces clean, such as vacuuming, dusting, and taking out trash. Include a schedule or rotation if applicable.]
- **Food and Groceries**: [Specify if food and groceries are shared or individual, including any arrangements for communal items or meals.]

4. Quiet Hours

- **Weekdays**: [Specify quiet hours, e.g., 10 PM to 7 AM, for activities that could disturb others.]
- **Weekends**: [Adjust quiet hours if necessary for weekends.]

5. Overnight Guests

- **Notice**: [Agree on how much advance notice should be given before a guest stays overnight.]
- **Frequency**: [Define how often guests can stay and for how long, e.g., no more than 3 consecutive nights and not more than twice a month.]
- **Behavior**: [Set expectations for the conduct of guests, especially during quiet hours.]

6. Study and Social Times

- **Study Environment**: [Agree on maintaining a conducive environment for studying during key times or during exam periods.]
- **Parties and Social Gatherings**: [Outline any guidelines or restrictions for hosting parties, including advance notice to roommates and responsibilities for clean-up.]

7. Personal Belongings

- **Borrowing Items**: [Specify guidelines on using or borrowing each other's belongings.]

- **Space**: [Define personal spaces (e.g., shelves, storage areas) and shared spaces and how they are to be used.]

8. Conflict Resolution

- **Discussion**: [Agree to discuss any conflicts or issues openly and respectfully with a goal to resolve them.]
- **Mediation**: [Specify a method for mediation or seeking external help if roommates cannot resolve an issue among themselves.]

9. Agreement Review and Modification

- **Review Schedule**: [Set times to review and, if necessary, revise the agreement, e.g., every semester.]
- **Signatures**: [All roommates sign and date the agreement, indicating consent and commitment to abide by it.]

Print it out, fill it in together, and stick it on your fridge. It's a visual reminder of your mutual pledges to make cohabitation as smooth as possible.

EFFECTIVE COMMUNICATION AND CONFLICT RESOLUTION

Living with someone inevitably means you'll run into a few bumps along the road. Whether it's over dishes left in the sink too long or someone's alarm clock going off at 5 AM every day, conflicts can arise from the quirkiest of situations. When conflicts do arise, the key is to communicate openly and respectfully. If something's bothering you, speak up sooner rather than later; don't let irritation build until you're ready to explode.

Starting off, identifying the root of conflicts is crucial. Sometimes what seems like a spat over unreturned clothes could actually be about respect for personal belongings or simply needing more space. Other times, tension might arise from different sleep schedules or study habits. It's about digging deep and asking the right questions, rather than making assumptions. Maybe your roomie's late-night guitar sessions aren't an attempt to drive you crazy but a way to unwind after a hectic day. Once you pinpoint the core issue, you're halfway to solving the puzzle.

Now, onto the golden skill of conflict resolution: active listening. This isn't just about nodding while your roommate talks; it's about genuinely trying to understand their perspective. It's putting yourself in their shoes and seeing the world from their dorm room window. When they're sharing, listen for feelings and needs rather than preparing your next argument in your head. Reflect back what you're hearing: "So, it sounds like you feel frustrated when I leave my stuff around because it makes the room feel cluttered?" This kind of mirroring can help both of you understand each other better and deflate many heated exchanges.

When you talk, focus on "I" statements—"I feel frustrated when dirty dishes are left in the sink" is easier to digest than "You're such a slob." Another example, "I feel overwhelmed by the loud music at night and I need some quiet in the evenings to decompress. Could we agree on quiet hours after 10 PM?" This approach shows you're not pointing fingers but rather looking for a solution that works for both.

Sometimes, despite your best efforts, you might hit a wall. When conflicts go round in circles, it might be time to bring in a neutral third party. Residential Advisors (RAs) are trained for exactly this kind of scenario. They can offer a fresh perspective and mediate discussions in a way that's fair to everyone involved. They're there to help you navigate these choppy waters and restore harmony. Knowing when to escalate a conflict to your RA or another authority figure shows maturity and commitment to resolving the issue, ensuring everyone can live together more comfortably.

Remember that living in a dorm is a unique blend of fun, challenges, and learning curves. By mastering the art of dorm etiquette, engaging in proactive conflict prevention, practicing effective communication, and knowing when to seek outside help, you're setting the stage for a harmonious living environment. These skills are not just about surviving dorm life; they're about enhancing your overall college experience, ensuring it's as enriching and enjoyable as possible.

THE ART OF MAKING DECISIONS AND LEARNING FROM MISTAKES

Imagine you're standing in front of two doors. Behind one, a peaceful library study session; behind the other, a spontaneous road trip with friends. Each has its perks, but you can only choose one. Here's where the classic pros and cons list comes into play. Jot down the immediate and long-term effects of each choice. Will one help you ace an upcoming exam? Will the other help you de-stress and make memories?

It's about mapping out the outcomes and seeing which aligns better with your goals. Think of it as your personal GPS system guiding you through the fog of options.

Now, let's talk about the elephant in the room: mistakes. Everyone makes them, but not everyone learns from them. In college, you're bound to stumble—maybe you over commit to clubs or underestimate the difficulty of a course. Instead of beating yourself up, look at each mistake as an opportunity to learn and grow. What went wrong? What can you do differently next time? Embracing your errors as learning opportunities broadens your understanding and hones your problem-solving skills, turning "oops" into a masterclass in personal development.

Building resilience is another key piece of the college survival kit. Think of it as your mental muscle—the stronger it is, the better you bounce back from setbacks. How do you build this muscle? Start by maintaining a positive outlook. When things go sideways, instead of spiraling into doom and gloom, try to find a silver lining. Did a failed project teach you a valuable lesson? Did a rejection from a club make you discover a new interest? Keeping your eyes on the growth can transform challenges into stepping stones, making you not just resilient, but unstoppable.

Lastly, the secret weapon in your decision-making arsenal: advice and mentoring. Whether it's a professor who sparks your intellectual curiosity or a senior student who knows the ropes, having a mentor is like having a live Google map for navigating college life. These relationships provide not just guidance but also encouragement and support. When faced with tough choices or unfamiliar situations, bouncing your thoughts off someone who's been in your shoes can provide clarity and direction. Remember, asking for advice isn't a sign of weakness; it's a strategy for success.

Navigating decision-making and learning from mistakes are crucial chapters in your college story. By honing your decision-making skills, embracing the lessons learned from missteps, building resilience, and seeking guidance, you're not just surviving college; you're mastering the art of thriving through life's ups and downs.

9

THE DO'S AND DON'TS OF COLLEGE PARTIES

College parties offer a diverse array of experiences, catering to a wide range of interests, making it all too easy to overindulge. Mastering the art of party navigation can be challenging. To navigate these social waters successfully, we'll establish some essential guidelines, ensuring your party experiences are positively unforgettable.

SAFETY FIRST

Think of going to a party like going on a road trip. You wouldn't start a journey without knowing your route and checking your car's safety, right? Apply the same logic to partying. Always plan how you're going to get back before you even step out. Whether it's ensuring you have a designated driver, the number for a reliable taxi service, or a fully charged phone to summon a ride-share, these details matter more than your outfit choice.

Always stick with your buddies. There's safety in numbers, and friends can look out for each other. Make a pact to leave together too. It's like having your own personal safety squad. And about your drinks—keep an eye on them. Never leave your drink unattended and watch it being made if possible. Unwanted substances can turn a night out into a nightmare. It's not just cautious; it's smart.

UNDERSTANDING CONSENT

Consent is the backbone of respect in any interaction, and it's crucial at parties where lines can sometimes get blurred. Always remember: consent is a clear, enthusiastic, ongoing yes, not the absence of a no. It can be withdrawn at any time, and being under the influence of alcohol or any other substance does not imply consent.

Make it a standard to engage in conversations about boundaries with people you meet. It's not only about respecting others' boundaries, but also about communicating your own. This clarity might sound like a buzzkill, but it actually clears the way for genuine fun that everyone is comfortable with. Respect and understanding create an environment where everyone can relax and enjoy without any underlying tensions.

MODERATION IS KEY

Here's where it gets real: balancing partying with your academics. It's tempting to think, "I can totally write that paper with a hangover," but let's be honest, no one does their best work with a pounding headache. Enjoying college life includes both acing your exams and having social fun, but the trick is to not let one sabotage the other.

Moderation is your best friend. It knows all about having a good time without next-day regrets. Set limits for yourself before the party starts and stick to them. It could be as simple as deciding beforehand how many drinks you'll have, or making sure you leave by a certain time to get enough sleep for your 9 AM class. Think of moderation as the savvy party-goer who knows how to dance the night away and still ace the test the next day.

NAVIGATING PEER PRESSURE

Peer pressure is like that one friend who always wants you to do something a bit outrageous. It's fun in small doses but can lead you astray if you're not careful. Remember, it's perfectly okay to say no. You're the boss of your life, and that means you get final say on what you do or don't do.

Don't hesitate to step away if a situation feels off. True friends will respect your choices, even if they tease you a bit. It's better to cope with a little FOMO than to deal with consequences that might throw off your game—academic or otherwise. Equip yourself with a few polite but firm ways to decline offers that don't align with your comfort zone. It's not about being a downer; it's about being in charge of your own experiences.

In summary, attending college parties can be a fun and memorable part of the college experience. Here's a review list of do's and don'ts to help you navigate these social events safely and responsibly:

DO'S

1. **Do Plan Ahead:** Know how you're getting to the party and how you'll get home. Consider arranging a designated driver or using public transportation.
2. **Do Stay with Friends:** Stick with your group to look out for each other's safety and well-being throughout the night.
3. **Do Know Your Limits:** Be aware of your alcohol tolerance and set limits for yourself to avoid overindulgence.
4. **Do Keep Your Drink with You:** Always keep an eye on your drink to prevent anyone from tampering with it.
5. **Do Charge Your Phone:** Ensure your phone is fully charged before you leave in case you need to call someone, order a ride, or navigate home.

DON'TS

1. **Don't Pressure Others:** Respect everyone's choice not to drink or participate in activities they're uncomfortable with.
2. **Don't Leave Drinks Unattended:** Never leave your drink unattended. If you lose sight of it, get a new one.
3. **Don't Drive Under the Influence:** Never drive if you've been drinking or allow friends to drive if they've been drinking.
4. **Don't Ignore Your Gut Feeling:** If something doesn't feel right, trust your instincts and leave.

5. **Don't Forget to Eat:** Eating before and during the party can help mitigate the effects of alcohol.

DRINKING RESPONSIBLY IN COLLEGE

Navigating the college social scene often includes encounters with alcohol, making it essential to understand how to drink responsibly. Responsible drinking means recognizing your limits and understanding the impact of alcohol on your body and mind. It's crucial to pace yourself, drink water between alcoholic beverages, and never drink on an empty stomach. Always have a plan for getting home safely, such as using a designated driver or ride-sharing service. Knowing when to say no is just as important as knowing your limits; never feel pressured to drink more than you are comfortable with. Remember, the goal is to enjoy yourself without compromising your safety or well-being.

UNDERSTANDING ALCOHOL CONTENT IN DRINKS

Not all alcoholic drinks are created equal. Different types of alcohol have varying amounts of ethanol, which is the active ingredient that causes intoxication. A standard drink in the United States typically contains about 14 grams of pure alcohol, which is found in 12 ounces of beer, 5 ounces of wine, or 1.5 ounces of distilled spirits like vodka or whiskey. It's easy to underestimate how much you are drinking, especially with mixed drinks or cocktails that can contain multiple shots of alcohol. Make sure you are aware of the alcohol content in your beverages so you can manage your intake more effectively.

HOW LONG ALCOHOL STAYS IN YOUR SYSTEM

The body metabolizes alcohol at a relatively constant rate, but this rate can vary slightly from person to person based on factors such as weight, age, sex, and overall health. On average, it takes about one hour for the body to metabolize the alcohol in one standard drink. However, this does not mean that you are completely sober after that time, as several drinks consumed in a short period can extend the time alcohol remains in your system. It's important to note that nothing can speed up this process—not coffee, cold showers, or energy drinks. Only time can reduce your blood alcohol concentration (BAC). This knowledge is crucial for planning activities and ensuring you do not engage in risky behaviors while still under the influence.

10

CAMPUS SAFETY AND PERSONAL SECURITY

First things first, let's talk about your new best friend on campus—the Campus Safety Office. No, they're not just there to scold you for losing your student ID again. These folks are the unsung heroes who ensure that your campus remains a safe haven. They offer a plethora of services, from safety escorts during those late-night study sessions to emergency call boxes strategically placed around campus. Picture this: It's late, you've just wrapped up a marathon library session, and the walk back to your dorm feels daunting. A safety escort can be your personal body-guard, ensuring you get back safely.

Pro tip? Learn the location of the campus safety office and familiarize yourself with the services they provide. Take a moment early in the semester to swing by their office. Ask questions, grab some safety brochures (it's more interesting than it sounds), and maybe even snag some contact numbers for quick access on your phone. It's like forming a friendship that not only makes you feel safer but actually keeps you safer. I teach several lab classes that have an exercise element to them, meaning high heart rates, high blood pressures, and the potential for injury. I make all of my students store the campus safety contact number in their cell phones at the beginning of the semester just in case an emergency situation arises. At let me tell you- it has!

Spend some time looking into apps like Circle of 6 or Safe-Trek which turn your device into a distress signal sender with just a few taps. These apps can alert your chosen contacts or even the authorities if you feel unsafe, sending them your location and other vital details. It's like having a panic button in your pocket.

Then there are personal safety devices that emit a loud sound to deter an attacker and draw attention. These gadgets are compact, often attachable to your keychain, and are as easy to use as pressing a button. It's like carrying a whistle, but much louder and more effective. Whether you're jogging early in the morning or crossing campus late at night, having these tools can make you feel like you have an emergency response team in your pocket.

Your new campus mantra should be: Be aware and take care. Staying safe is often about trusting your instincts and making smart choices about where you go and when. Avoid shortcuts through poorly lit or secluded areas. Stick to well-traveled paths, and always be aware of your surroundings—no getting lost in your playlist or deep in a texting session while walking. Keep your head up and your eyes open. Reflecting on my college years, I remember the long runs I used to take through various neighborhoods and areas of town. As a young woman without a cell phone (yes, I am aging myself but we did not have cell phones back then), I now look back at the risks I unknowingly took, and I realize that I would not feel comfortable doing the same today.

Nighttime on campus doesn't have to be a no-go zone if you keep your wits about you. Walk with purpose and confidence. If you ever feel uneasy, go into a campus building and call a friend or the campus safety office for an escort. Remember, lighting is your ally. Stay in well-lit areas, and if you notice a burned-out streetlamp, report it.

EMERGENCY PREPAREDNESS

Finally, let's talk about being prepared for emergencies. This isn't just about knowing where the exits are in each of your classrooms (though that's a great start). It's about understanding the specific procedures for different emergencies—fires, severe weather, and other campus threats. Most colleges have alert systems in place—make sure you're signed up to receive these alerts, whether they're sent via text, email, or over loudspeakers. I am set up to receive a text, e-mail, and phone call in the case of a campus emergency. If an emergency arises during class, a bold message appears on all projection screens and network computers, alerting everyone on campus of the emergency.

Take the time to familiarize yourself with evacuation routes and emergency assembly points. Participate in any drills that are conducted on campus or in your dorms. And keep an emergency kit in your dorm room—basic supplies like water, non-perishable food, a flashlight, and a first-aid kit can be a lifesaver in unexpected situations.

INTERACTIVE ELEMENT: SAFETY QUIZ

Are You Prepared? Take This Quick Safety Quiz!

- Do you know the location of the nearest emergency exit in your classroom/building/dorm?
- Can you name two services provided by your campus safety office?
- Have you downloaded any personal safety apps on your phone? If so, which ones?
- Do you know where to go or what to do in case of severe weather or other emergencies on campus?

Taking a few moments to answer these questions can help you gauge your readiness and perhaps highlight areas where you might need to beef up your safety smarts. Remember, being prepared isn't about being paranoid—it's about being empowered. And that's a key part of ensuring your college experience is not only fun and enriching but safe too.

FOSTERING RESPECTFUL RELATIONSHIPS

Navigating college relationships—whether platonic, romantic, or somewhere in between—calls for a solid understanding of one crucial concept: consent. Think of consent not just as a formal agreement but as the golden rule of all interactions. It's the clear, enthusiastic "yes" that should precede any advance, physical or otherwise. Consent is active, not passive. It's ongoing, meaning it can be revoked at any moment, and it must be informed, meaning everyone involved understands exactly what they're agreeing to without any influence of drugs, alcohol, or pressure.

In the intricate network of relationships, effective communication serves as the essential link that binds all interactions. It's about being clear with your words and attentive to the words of others. More than just talking, effective communication involves listening—really listening—to understand others' boundaries and comfort levels. And it's not just about what's said out loud. Non-verbal cues, those subtle signals like body language and facial expressions, are just as important. They can often tell you more about a person's comfort and consent than words ever could. Imagine you're at a party; someone leans away as you step closer, they might not say it, but their body is whispering, "This is my space."

Bystander intervention is another powerful tool in your relationship toolkit. It's about looking out for each other. If you see someone in a situation that doesn't seem right—maybe a friend seems uncomfortable with someone's advances at a party—it's your cue to step in. But how? It could be as simple as striking up a conversation with the person involved, allowing them a chance to step away. Or perhaps, it's asking directly if they're okay, thereby giving them an opportunity to voice their discomfort. Sometimes, it might mean involving others like security or event staff.

Lastly, the support systems on campus and in the community are invaluable. Whether someone has experienced assault or just feels uneasy about an interaction, knowing where to turn for help is crucial. Most colleges have counseling centers, health services, and legal aid, all equipped to handle such situations confidentially and compassionately. These resources are there to provide support, guidance, and, when necessary, intervention. They ensure that every student knows they're not alone, that they have a network of professionals ready to stand by their side.

Navigating relationships in college can be complex, but with a clear understanding of consent, effective communication, active bystander intervention, and robust support systems, students can foster respectful and healthy interactions. These are not just skills for college but for life, ensuring that all relationships are built on mutual respect and understanding.

As we close this chapter on personal safety and respect, remember that these lessons are pillars not just for your time in college but for all the years that follow. Reviewing what we have discussed, here are 5 strategies for staying safe on a college campus:

1. **Stay Aware of Your Surroundings**: Always be conscious of your environment, especially when walking around campus late at night. Keep your head up, avoid distractions like your phone, and stay in well-lit areas. If you ever feel unsafe, trust your instincts and seek a safer location.

2. **Use Campus Safety Resources**: Familiarize yourself with the safety services your campus offers, such as campus escort services, emergency call stations, and campus security phone numbers. Don't hesitate to use these resources whenever you feel a need.

3. **Keep Your Living Area Secure**: Always lock your dorm room or apartment, even if you're just leaving for a few minutes. Do not lend out your keys or access card, and be cautious about who you let into your living space.

4. **Practice Safe Socializing**: When attending parties or social events, go with friends and look out for each other. Be cautious with alcohol consumption, and never leave your drink unattended. Have a plan for getting home safely, such as a designated driver or a ride-share app that you can trust.

5. **Stay Connected**: Keep your phone charged and within reach when you're out, and let someone know where you're going and when you expect to return. Having a friend or family member aware of your schedule can add an extra layer of safety.

11

MENTAL HEALTH AWARENESS

Surveys indicate that nearly one in three college students report having experienced debilitating depression, while more than 50% have felt overwhelming anxiety during their academic journey. Additionally, a considerable number of students face difficulties such as stress, sleep disturbances, and eating disorders, all of which can severely impact their academic performance, social interactions, and overall quality of life. I tell you these statistics to help bring awareness to the importance of recognizing and addressing mental health proactively to support your success and well-being.

RECOGNIZING SIGNS OF STRESS AND ANXIETY

You know those moments when it seems like you're drinking from a firehose due to the amount of homework and personal obligations? Or those nights when worries about exams keep your mind racing all night? That's stress and anxiety knocking at your door. Understanding how to identify and manage these intrusive feelings as these emotions can significantly impact your academic performance and overall well-being.

Stress often manifests through physical symptoms such as headaches, muscle tension, fatigue, and sleep disturbances. You might also experience emotional symptoms, including feelings of overwhelm, irritability, or a general sense of being out of control. Anxiety, while related to stress, brings its own set of symptoms such as excessive worrying, restlessness, and a tendency to anticipate the worst outcomes. It's not uncommon for anxiety to also cause difficulties in concentration, which can directly affect your ability to study and perform academically.

It is important for you to observe your own patterns of behavior and physical responses, especially during difficult academic periods, such as midterms or finals. Psychological symptoms might include a persistent sense of dread, panic attacks, or avoiding social situations due to feelings of fear and apprehension. Recognizing these symptoms early can help you seek the appropriate help, such as counseling services offered by your college, or developing your own coping strategies.

Here are several effective strategies that can help you manage stress and anxiety:

1. **Mindfulness and Meditation**: Practicing mindfulness and meditation can significantly reduce stress and anxiety by fostering a state of awareness and relaxation.
2. **Regular Exercise**: Physical activity is a proven stress reliever. It not only helps in reducing the

levels of the body's stress hormones, such as adrenaline and cortisol, but it also stimulates the production of endorphins, chemicals in the brain that are the body's natural painkillers and mood elevators.

3. **Time Management Skills**: Effective time management can alleviate stress by helping you avoid the panic of last-minute cramming and deadlines. Learning to prioritize tasks and break projects into manageable steps can prevent overwhelming situations.

4. **Social Support**: Whether it's friends, family, or college support groups, being able to share your feelings and concerns with others who listen and offer advice can be profoundly comforting.

5. **Adequate Sleep**: Sleep and mental health are closely connected. College students often sacrifice sleep for academics or social life, but insufficient sleep can exacerbate stress and anxiety. Establishing a regular sleep schedule and practicing good sleep hygiene can improve both your mood and academic performance.

6. **Balanced Diet**: Eating a healthy, balanced diet can affect your mental health positively. Foods rich in vitamins, minerals, and antioxidants nourish the brain and protect it from oxidative stress, which can be induced by stress and can lead to anxiety.

7. **Professional Help**: Sometimes, professional help is needed to manage stress and anxiety effectively. Counseling services and therapy provided by colleges can offer crucial support and coping strategies.

8. **Relaxation Techniques**: Try deep breathing exercises, progressive muscle relaxation, or yoga to reduce stress and enhance your sense of well-being.

9. **Mood diary**—Jot down a few notes about how you're feeling each day. Spot patterns and triggers. Is the thought of upcoming exams turning your mood barometer stormy? Are back-to-back social commitments leaving you drained?

10. **Stress journal**- Rate your stress level daily on a scale from 1 to 10. Seeing a week filled with 8s and 9s? That's your cue to step up your self-care game.

INTERACTIVE ELEMENT: MINDFULNESS MINUTE EXERCISE

To get a real feel for how mindfulness can dial down your stress, here's a quick exercise you can do anywhere, anytime. It's called the Mindfulness Minute:

1. Find a comfortable spot to sit or stand.
2. Set a timer for one minute on your phone or watch.
3. Close your eyes, take a deep breath, and gradually tune into the sensation of breathing. Feel the air moving in and out of your lungs, the rise and fall of your chest.
4. If your mind wanders (and it will), gently bring your focus back to your breath.
5. When the timer goes off, slowly bring your attention back to your surroundings.

Notice a bit of mental fog lifting? That's mindfulness in action—small moments can lead to big changes in your stress levels. Integrating exercises like this into your daily routine can help keep stress and anxiety in check, making your college experience not just bearable, but enjoyable.

IMPACT ON ACADEMIC PERFORMANCE

High stress levels can significantly undermine your focus, making study sessions far less effective. Similarly, your memory may suffer, causing important information to escape you when you need it most, such as during exams. But here's the kicker: it's not just about poorer grades. Chronic stress and anxiety can lead to burnout, where even the simplest tasks feel impossible. That's why keeping your mental health in check is key to maintaining not just your GPA but your overall zest for college life.

So, as you flip through this chapter and arm yourself with strategies to tackle stress and anxiety, remember: college is not just about surviving academically or socially—it's about thriving emotionally and mentally. With the right tools and a proactive approach, you can ensure that your college years are as enriching and fulfilling as they are meant to be.

CAMPUS RESOURCES FOR MENTAL HEALTH SUPPORT

Your campus is like a small city equipped with its own health care system, specifically designed to keep you thriving physically, mentally, as well as academically. Knowing the resources you have available to you as a college student can make a world of difference.

Your college likely has a counseling center, and this should be your first pit stop if you're feeling overwhelmed. These centers typically offer a range of services, from one-on-one counseling sessions to stress management workshops, all tailored to the unique needs of students. To get started, a simple visit to your school's website or a quick inquiry at the student services office can point you in the right direction. Don't hesitate to drop by the counseling center either. It's there for you, and making the most of these services is as smart as hitting the library before exams.

Now, let's chat about peer support groups. These are spaces where students can come together under the guidance of a trained facilitator to share experiences and support each other. Whether it's stress, homesickness, or more specific issues like dealing with anxiety or depression, these groups offer a safe environment where you can talk openly and find comfort in the fact that you're not alone in how you feel. The beauty of peer support lies in its basis of shared experiences; sometimes, just knowing that there are others who understand exactly what you're going through can be incredibly comforting. To find these groups, keep an eye on campus bulletin boards, social media platforms, or the university's event calendar where meetings are often advertised.

In cases where you might need immediate help, knowing about emergency mental health services is crucial. Most campuses have protocols in place for urgent situations, which can include on-call counselors, crisis hot-lines, and links to local mental health services. These resources are vital in times of crisis and can provide immediate support and intervention. Familiarize yourself with these services at the beginning of each school year. You can even program the campus police or crisis hot-line into your cellphone.

Building a personal support network is another essential strategy. This network can include friends, family, favorite professors, or even residential advisors. Having a go-to group of people who know you and can offer support when you're down or stressed can make all the difference. Cultivate these relationships; attend faculty office hours to build rapport with professors, participate in community events to deepen friendships, and keep in touch with family, whether through weekly phone calls or text updates.

Navigating your mental health resources might not be the first thing on your mind when you start college, but knowing where to turn when you need support is as crucial as knowing your major. Equip yourself with this knowledge early on, and you'll be better prepared to handle whatever college throws your way, ensuring that your college years are not only successful but also healthy and happy.

12

PHYSICAL HEALTH AND NUTRITION

L et's be real, eating healthy on a college budget is often seen as a mythical feat, right up there with getting a good night's sleep during finals week. But what if I told you that you can eat well without breaking the bank or resorting to a diet of instant ramen and vending machine snacks?

BUDGET-FRIENDLY NUTRITION

The secret to eating well on a shoestring budget isn't just about hunting for the cheapest eats. It's about making smart choices that maximize nutrition without draining your funds. Start with the basics—beans, rice, oats, and frozen veggies. These staples are not only affordable but also versatile enough to form the backbone of countless meals. Buying in bulk can also save you a packet, especially for non-perishables. Don't shy away from using coupons, and keep an eye on sales at your local grocery store—planning your shopping around what's discounted can lead to significant savings.

Meal planning is the secret to managing your nutrition and your budget. By planning your meals for the week, you avoid the trap of impulse buys and last-minute unhealthy choices. Start with a simple chart or use a meal planning app to map out your meals. Make sure each meal has a good balance of proteins, carbs, and fats.

Preparation is key. Dedicate a couple of hours each week to prep your meals. Cook in bulk and use your fridge creatively. Storing individual meal portions saves time and reduces waste. It's like having your own personal fast food, ready whenever you need it, minus the unhealthy part.

Understanding the basics of nutrition can arm you with the knowledge to make informed food choices. Carbohydrates, proteins, and fats are your body's primary energy sources, each playing unique roles. Carbs are your body's main fuel source, proteins are essential for repair and growth, and fats are vital for long-term energy and cell function. Aim for a balance to support both your physical and cognitive functions—yes, your brain loves nutrients too!

Also, don't forget about micronutrients—vitamins and minerals like iron, calcium, and vitamins A, C, and D are crucial for everything from immune function to bone health. Snack on fruits, nuts, and seeds, as they are packed with nutrients and easy to eat on the go.

Navigating the campus dining halls can feel like a nutrition minefield. But fear not, it's possible to make healthy choices amidst the maze of pizza slices, french fries, unlimited ice cream, and pasta stations. Most dining halls offer a salad bar—load up on the greens and top them with a variety of veggies, beans, and a simple olive oil and vinegar dressing. Steer clear of creamy dressings and go easy on cheese and croutons. Opt for grilled, steamed, or baked options instead of fried. And if you're in doubt about the best choices, don't hesitate to chat with the dining staff. They can provide valuable insights into the day's healthiest options.

When eating out or ordering in, look for restaurants with healthier options. Many places now offer whole-grain, low-fat, and low-sodium choices. And remember, portion control is your friend. Consider sharing a meal with a friend or packing half to take home for another meal.

INTERACTIVE ELEMENT: GROCERY SHOPPING LIST TEMPLATE

To help you put all this into practice, here's a handy template for your next grocery shopping trip. Customize it based on your preferences and dietary needs:

- **Proteins**: Chicken breast, tofu, eggs, canned tuna, nuts
- **Carbs**: Brown rice, whole wheat pasta, quinoa, sweet potatoes
- **Vegetables**: Spinach, broccoli, carrots, bell peppers (fresh or frozen)
- **Fruits**: Apples, bananas, oranges, frozen berries
- **Dairy/Dairy Alternatives**: Greek yogurt, almond milk, cheese
- **Snacks**: Almonds, sunflower seeds, hummus
- **Condiments/Spices**: Olive oil, vinegar, mustard, black pepper, turmeric

100 | CRUSH YOUR FRESHMAN YEAR

This list can guide your shopping and ensure you have various foods to keep your meals interesting and nutritious. Stick it on your fridge or save it on your phone for easy access during your shopping trips.

SIMPLE AND EFFECTIVE EXERCISE ROUTINES FOR BUSY STUDENTS

Let's face it, squeezing in gym time between classes, study sessions, and the occasional social life can seem daunting. However, keeping active doesn't need to be a chore or require fancy equipment. You can actually sneak in some pretty effective exercise moves between your daily activities, and here's how.

Incorporating physical activity into your daily routine can be as simple as switching up your commute. If you live on campus, try walking or biking to your classes instead of taking the shuttle. Those extra steps add up, and you get to enjoy some fresh air—it's a win-win! For those of you living off-campus, consider getting off a bus stop earlier or parking further away. It's about making movement a natural part of your day, not an extra task on your to-do list.

Even your dorm room can double as a mini-gym. A quick 10-minute workout in the morning can kick start your metabolism and boost your energy for the day. Simple body weight exercises like push-ups, sit-ups, and squats don't require much space but can make a significant impact on your fitness. And let's not forget the power of stretching— taking a few minutes to stretch after a long study session not only breaks the monotony but also helps reduce muscle tension and fatigue.

Speaking of the campus, have you explored the recreational facilities available at your university? Most campuses are equipped with sports centers that offer a range of fitness programs—from yoga classes to swimming pools and even rock climbing walls. These facilities are usually free or discounted for students, so make sure you're taking full advantage of them. If you have a gap in your class schedule, plan ahead and bring your workout clothes to get in a quick exercise session in between classes. Joining an intramural sports team is another fun way to stay active and meet new people. Whether it's ultimate frisbee, soccer, or even Pickleball, getting involved in campus sports can be a fantastic outlet for both physical activity and some healthy competition.

Online fitness resources have exploded in recent years, offering everything from high-intensity interval training (HIIT) to Pilates, all streamable right to your laptop or smartphone. Platforms like YouTube have countless fitness channels with workouts that range from 5 minutes to an hour, many of which require no equipment. Apps like FitOn and Nike Training Club also offer free workouts tailored to all fitness levels. So, next time you're binge-watching a series, why not watch a quick fitness video and move along?

Lastly, it's crucial to recognize the role of regular physical activity in managing stress and improving mental health. Exercise releases endorphins, often known as the body's natural feel-good hormones. This can be incredibly beneficial during stressful periods like midterms or finals. Regular physical activity has been shown to improve mood, reduce feelings of anxiety, and even enhance sleep quality—critical factors in maintaining overall mental health.

So, even if you're juggling a jam-packed schedule, integrating some form of physical activity into your routine can significantly enhance your college experience. It keeps your body healthy and your mind sharp, helping you navigate through your college years with energy and positivity. Remember, exercise shouldn't be a burden—it's there to uplift you, physically and mentally.

As we wrap up this chapter on physical health and nutrition, remember that taking care of your body is just as important as feeding your mind. Whether it's choosing the right foods or finding ways to stay active, a balanced approach to physical health can significantly enhance your academic performance and overall well-being. Next, we'll explore effective budget management strategies, ensuring that your financial health is also on track for success. Keep turning the pages; there's more to learn and more ways to ensure your college years are as healthy and fulfilling as possible!

INTERACTIVE ELEMENT: HEALTH TRACKER CHECKLIST

To keep you on track, here's a simple health tracker checklist. Tick off these tasks to stay on top of your game:

- **Annual Check-Up**: Booked and done? Check.
- **Exercise Routine**: Found your fit? Check.
- **Balanced Diet**: Keeping it colorful? Check.
- **Sleep Routine**: Consistently catching those Z's? Check.
- **Mental Health Resource List**: Compiled your go-to helpers? Check.

This checklist isn't just a to-do list; it's your personal cheat sheet to staying healthy, happy, and wise in the ways of independent living. Stick it on your fridge, your wall, or keep it on your phone—somewhere you'll see it and keep yourself in check, literally.

13

BUDGETING AND MANAGING
EXPENSES

First things first, let's lay out what you've got coming in versus what's going out. Start by pinpointing every source of income. This might include money from part-time jobs, parental support, scholarships, grants, and if you're one of the lucky few, maybe some savings. It's important to get a clear picture of your total monthly income to know how to budget successfully.

Next up, list all of your expenses. From the big-ticket items like tuition, rent, and meal plans to the sneakier little costs that can add up, like streaming subscriptions, midnight pizza orders, and yes, those coffee runs. Categorize your expenses into 'fixed' (those that don't change month to month, like rent) and 'variable' (the ones that can fluctuate, like groceries or entertainment). This gives you a bird's-eye view of where your money is going, making it easier to spot areas where you can cut back if needed.

Allocate funds for your non-negotiables first—tuition, books, housing, and food. These are your financial foundation; everything else is built on ensuring these are covered. Once your essentials are accounted for, you can divvy up what's left. Maybe you set aside a portion for social activities (because all work and no play is not how we roll), a bit for personal expenses (like clothes and, dare we say, a decent haircut?), and don't forget to add to your savings, even if it's just a few dollars each month.

TRACKING SPENDING

You need to know where every dollar is going. This is where budgeting apps come into play. Apps like Mint, YNAB (You Need A Budget), or even a simple spreadsheet can help you keep tabs on your spending in real time. They can categorize your expenses, send you alerts when you're overspending, and even provide insights on your spending patterns over time. Make it a habit to review your expenses regularly. Seeing the numbers can sometimes be a wake-up call, but more importantly, it helps you stay in control and make adjustments before things spiral.

Your budget isn't set in stone. As you go through the semester, you'll find that some months are pricier than others (hello, textbook season), and sometimes, unexpected expenses pop up (weekend road trips, flat tire).

Regularly revisiting your budget allows you to tweak it based on what's actually happening in your financial life. Maybe you decide to cut back on eating out to save for a concert ticket, or perhaps you pick up a side gig to cover a surprise expense. The key is to stay flexible and proactive, ensuring your budget evolves as your circumstances do.

INTERACTIVE ELEMENT: MONTHLY BUDGET TRACKER

To give you a head start, here's a simple budget tracker you can use to monitor your monthly finances:

Monthly Budget Tracker Template

Income:

1. Part-time Job: $ _____
2. Scholarships/Grants: $ _____
3. Parental/Family Support: $ _____
4. Savings: $ _____
5. Other Sources (Specify): $ _____
6. Total Income: $ _____

Expenses:

1. Rent/Housing: $ _____
2. Utilities (electric, water, internet): $ _____
3. Groceries/Food: $ _____
4. Transportation (gas, public transit): $ _____
5. School Supplies (books, materials): $ _____
6. Personal Care (laundry, toiletries): $ _____
7. Entertainment (movies, dining out): $ _____
8. Health (insurance, medical bills): $ _____
9. Other (Specify): $ _____

Total Expenses: $ _____

Monthly Overview:

- **Total Income:** $ _____
- **Total Expenses:** $ _____
- **Balance (Income - Expenses):** $ _____

Savings Goals:

1. **Short-term Goal (e.g., new laptop):** $ _____
2. **Long-term Goal (e.g., study abroad):** $ _____

Notes:

- **Adjustments Needed for Next Month:**
- (List any changes you plan to make to your budget, such as reducing spending in certain categories or finding ways to increase income.)

This template is your starting point. Adjust the categories and amounts according to your own income and expenses. Track your spending throughout the month, and at the end, sit down and see how you did. Over or under? Adjust as needed for the next month.

SAVING MONEY: TIPS AND TRICKS FOR COLLEGE STUDENTS

Who says you have to break the bank to enjoy college? Not me! Let's dive into some savvy strategies to keep more of your hard-earned cash in your pocket. Starting with student discounts—these are the college student's secret weapon for stretching those dollars. You can snag discounts on everything from software and subscriptions to movies and public transport. Your student ID is like a golden ticket—use it everywhere! Many tech companies offer hefty discounts on software that can be crucial for your studies. Adobe, Microsoft, and even Apple give you price breaks just for being a student. And don't forget about streaming services like Spotify and Hulu often bundling services at a discount for students. For transportation, check out local transit options; many cities offer reduced or even free fares for students. Always ask if a student discount is available—you'll be surprised how often the answer is yes.

Textbooks- they can suck your wallet dry faster than a vacuum on steroids. But fear not, there are ways to dodge those sky-high prices. Buying used textbooks can save you a bundle. Check out online platforms like Amazon, Chegg, or your university's Facebook groups where students often sell their old books at steep discounts. Renting textbooks is another wallet-friendly option. Services like Chegg or your campus bookstore often offer rental options that cost a fraction of buying new. And let's not overlook the power of the library. Many textbooks are available to borrow, and while you might not get to write in the margins, your bank account will thank you.

Speaking of saving, let's chat about the importance of an emergency fund. It's like your financial safety net, ready to catch you when life throws you a curveball—a surprise car repair, an unexpected trip home, or even just a lost phone. Start small; even a few dollars from each paycheck or financial aid refund can build up over time. Open a savings account that's a bit harder to access than your checking—out of sight, out of mind, but there when you need it. Aim to save enough to cover at least a month of living expenses. It might seem like a drag now, but when you hit a bump, you'll be patting yourself on the back.

And if you're finding your wallet a bit too light, consider earning some extra cash. Part-time jobs are the classic choice —campus jobs are particularly convenient as they're often flexible around your class schedule. But don't stop there. Gig economy jobs like driving for ride-sharing services, delivering food, or freelancing in areas like writing, graphic design, or tutoring can fit into odd hours outside your classes. Internships, especially paid ones, are another fantastic way to earn money while also gaining valuable experience in your field of study.

Navigating your finances in college doesn't have to mean living off ramen noodles (unless you want to, of course). With the right tricks up your sleeve—from leveraging student discounts and buying used textbooks to building an emergency fund and grabbing part-time gigs—you can keep your finances healthy without missing out on the fun parts of college life. So keep these tips in your back pocket, and watch your savings grow—your future self will thank you.

14

UNDERSTANDING STUDENT LOANS AND GRANTS

We are diving into the world of student loans and grants—a realm where terms like "subsidized" and "FAFSA" roam free, and where understanding the fine print can save you a ton of stress (and cash) down the road. Whether you're eyeing those loan applications with a mix of dread and necessity, or you're just curious about what financial aid options are out there, I've got you covered. Let's demystify the beast, shall we?

TYPES OF STUDENT LOANS

First off, let's tackle the different types of student loans because not all loans are created equal, and knowing the difference can impact your wallet big time. You've got two main players in the game: federal loans and private loans. Federal loans are like the steady, reliable friend who's got your back, offering fixed interest rates and flexible repayment terms. They're funded by the government and include options like Direct Subsidized Loans (where the government pays the interest while you're in school) and Direct Unsubsidized Loans (where you're on the hook for the interest, but you can defer it until after graduation).

Then there are private loans, the wild cards. These are offered by banks, credit unions, and other financial institutions, and their terms can vary widely. Interest rates might be fixed or variable (read: they can change), and they often require a credit check. Think of private loans as a last resort —like calling your eccentric uncle for a ride because your car's in the shop. It'll do in a pinch, but you'd rather avoid it if you can.

And here's where it gets a bit more complex with interest rates. Imagine you're borrowing $10,000. With a fixed interest rate, you know exactly how much you'll need to pay back, just like knowing the exact cost of a concert ticket. Variable rates, however, can fluctuate, kind of like gas prices, making it trickier to predict your total costs over time.

APPLYING FOR STUDENT LOANS

Navigating the application process for student loans is like assembling IKEA furniture—follow the instructions carefully, and you'll end up with a sturdy bed (or a manageable loan). It all starts with the FAFSA (Free Application for Federal Student Aid). It is your gateway to all federal loans, grants, and work-study funds. Filling it out can feel a bit like a tax return, requiring details about your finances and your family's. But it's worth the effort because it could open the door to financial aid that doesn't need to be repaid—like grants and scholarships.

Once you submit your FAFSA, you'll receive a financial aid offer from your college, which might include federal student loans. Here's where you need to put on your detective hat. Scrutinize the offer, understand the terms, and only accept what you need. Remember, every dollar borrowed is a dollar that needs to be paid back—with interest.

REPAYMENT PLANS AND OPTIONS

Federal loans offer several repayment plans that can help keep your payments affordable. These range from the Standard Repayment Plan, which stretches your payments over 10 years, to income-driven repayment plans, which adjust your monthly payments based on how much money you make. It's like a sliding scale for your debt, designed to keep your payments within reach.

And here's a beacon of hope if you're entering certain professions: loan forgiveness programs. For instance, the Public Service Loan Forgiveness program might erase your remaining debt after you make 10 years of qualifying payments while working in public service. It's like a marathon where crossing the finish line could mean saying goodbye to your student debt.

UNDERSTANDING THE LONG-TERM IMPACT

Grasping the long-term impact of taking out student loans is crucial. It's tempting to focus on the immediate relief they provide for your tuition bills, but remember, this is a long-term relationship, not a summer fling. Think about how your future self, maybe ten years from now, will handle the monthly payments. Will you be okay with a chunk of your paycheck going toward student loans? It's essential to borrow only what you need and consider your future income potential when deciding how much to take on.

Consider this: taking out loans is a bit like investing in your own future. You're betting on yourself, your career, and your ability to pay back the debt. It's an investment that should be made wisely and with a clear understanding of the terms and your own financial reality. Treat it with the same seriousness and optimism as you would any significant life decision, because, in many ways, that's exactly what it is.

HOW TO FIND AND APPLY FOR GRANTS AND SCHOLARSHIPS

Whether you're a brainiac, an athlete, a budding artist, or someone who's been actively involved in community service, there's likely a scholarship or grant with your name on it. But like any treasure worth having, it requires some digging.

First up, where to look? Your starting point should always be the federal and state grant programs. These are the big players in the financial aid game, and they often have the most significant pots of money. Fill out your FAFSA, as this is your golden ticket to accessing these funds. But don't stop there. Your own college is a treasure trove of scholarships and grants, often based on merit, financial need, field of study, or some unique combination of factors. Pop into your financial aid office, or better yet, dive into your college's website to unearth these opportunities.

Expand your horizon to external scholarships from private organizations, companies, and non-profits. These can range from small, niche awards to large national competitions, covering a vast array of criteria from academic excellence to unique personal hobbies. Websites like Fastweb, Scholarships.com, and the College Board offer searchable databases where you can filter scholarships by your qualifications, interests, and even specific criteria like your background or chosen major.

Now, onto eligibility and requirements—this part's crucial. Each scholarship or grant has its own set of rules. Some might require a certain GPA, others might look for community service or leadership experience, and some might just want you to write an essay about your life story. Make sure you read the fine print. Missing a small detail can be the difference between scoring that scholarship and missing out.

So, you've found the perfect grant or scholarship. How do you clinch it? Here's where you need to channel your inner marketer and sell yourself. Most applications require an essay, and this is your chance to shine. Tell your story in a way that captures attention. Be genuine, be heartfelt, and most importantly, be clear about how this scholarship will help you achieve your dreams. And don't forget the polish— no typos or grammatical errors, please. Have someone else read your application to catch any mistakes and give feedback.

Letters of recommendation are another cornerstone of a strong application. Choose your recommenders wisely— pick teachers, mentors, or bosses who not only know you well but also are familiar with your accomplishments and can speak to your character and abilities. Give them plenty of time to write the recommendation, and provide them with context about what the scholarship is for so they can tailor their letter to it.

Lastly, keep an eye on the deadlines. Missing a deadline is like showing up to the party after everyone's gone home—no matter how good your invitation is, it won't matter if it's late. Set reminders, mark calendars, do whatever it takes to get your application in on time.

Maintaining eligibility is the final piece of the puzzle. Most scholarships require you to meet certain criteria continuously, like maintaining a specific GPA or participating in community service. View it as an ongoing commitment, not a one-off checkbox. Staying eligible means staying engaged, keeping your grades up, and continuing to meet whatever other requirements the scholarship has set.

Navigating the waters of grants and scholarships can feel overwhelming, but with the right approach, it's entirely manageable. Think of each application as a step towards graduating without a mountain of debt, a step towards your dreams. So stay persistent, stay meticulous, and let's make this happen.

Moving forward, remember, the journey through college isn't just about maintaining grades or securing financial aid —it's about growing, learning, and preparing for the world beyond campus. In the next chapter, we'll explore how to select the right major for you, aligning your academic pursuits with your career ambitions.

15

SELECTING YOUR MAJOR

A re you someone who thrives in a fast-paced, competitive environment? Maybe a dash of business or entrepreneurship is in your future. Or perhaps you're more about helping others and making a tangible difference, which could point you towards careers in education, healthcare, or social work. This isn't about locking in a life path— it's about exploring the possibilities. Your career interests might change, and that's totally okay. College is the perfect time for a little career exploration experimentation.

SELF-ASSESSMENT TOOLS

Before you can choose your major, you need to know yourself a bit better. Self-assessment tools are here to help with that.

Start with personality tests like the Myers-Briggs Type Indicator or the Strong Interest Inventory. These tools can give you a clearer picture of your strengths and interests, and how they translate into academic and career paths. For example, if you're someone who scores high on creativity and people skills, a major in communications or marketing might be your alley. Or, if you're detail-oriented and love structure, think about accounting or engineering.

Next, there are skill assessments. This isn't just about what you're good at; it's about what you enjoy doing. Maybe you're great at math, but the thought of solving equations all-day makes you want to run for the hills. Skills assessments help you identify not only what you excel in, but also what activities give you energy rather than drain it. Websites like CareerOneStop offer skills assessments that you can take for free. They provide a detailed report that aligns your skills with potential majors and careers—pretty handy, right?

RESEARCHING MAJORS

Researching majors is about understanding what you're signing up for. Start by looking at the courses required for each major. If the thought of sitting through 'Quantitative Statistical Methods' makes you queasy, then a major in Sociology might be more your speed than Economics.

Don't stop at just the course titles; dig into the syllabi if you can. Many universities have these available online, or you could email a professor to ask about typical assignments. Are there lots of group projects? Heavy on the readings? Knowing this can help you decide if it's something you'd actually enjoy or if it just sounded cool on the brochure.

Also, explore the career trajectories. While you're not locking yourself into a specific job, it's good to know what fields are common for graduates in your potential major. University career centers and websites like the Bureau of Labor Statistics can give you a glimpse into future job markets, typical earnings, and more. This could be the deciding factor between two majors or open your eyes to possibilities you hadn't considered.

TALKING TO ADVISORS AND FACULTY

If someone asked me to give college students only one piece of advice, I would say this, "Talk to your academic advisor and your professors regularly." Meeting with your academic advisor and faculty within your department is a game-changer. These individuals know their stuff and can offer you insider tips that aren't found on the website.

Set up a meeting with an academic advisor to discuss your interests and career goals as soon as possible. They can help you map out potential academic paths and clarify any confusion about prerequisites or dual degree options. Don't forget to reach out to faculty members, especially those teaching in the areas you're interested in. Ask about their research, the kinds of students who thrive in their programs, and opportunities for internships or projects. This can give you a real taste of what studying that major might be like.

UTILIZING CAREER SERVICES

Don't overlook your campus career services. Career services can offer you workshops, career fairs, and one-on-one counseling sessions. It's like having a personal career coach. They can help you refine your resume, prep for interviews, and even connect you with job opportunities.

Career fairs, in particular, are golden opportunities to network with potential employers. You want to make a good impression quickly—dress sharp, have your elevator pitch polished, and bring copies of your resume. And follow up! Sending a thank-you note after a career fair can set you apart from the crowd. It shows you're serious about your career and value the connections you've made.

CONSIDERING DOUBLE MAJORS AND MINORS

If choosing one major is tough, why on earth would you choose two? Double majoring or picking up a minor can expand your knowledge base and make you more versatile in the job market.

But it's not all positive—double majors mean a tighter schedule and more work, and it's not for everyone. Weigh the benefits against the added stress. Will it significantly boost your career prospects? Do the fields complement each other? For instance, majoring in both English and Marketing could give you a serious edge in fields like advertising or media.

Minors are a great option if you're mostly committed to one area but have a strong interest in another. It allows you to develop another area of expertise and can make your education feel more customized to your interests.

Choosing a major (or two) is a big decision, but it's also an exciting one. It's your chance to shape your college experience and pave the way for your future career. Use these tools and tips to help you make a choice that feels right—not just for the job market, but for you. After all, college is about finding your path, and sometimes, that starts with choosing which courses to take.

THE IMPACT OF YOUR MAJOR ON YOUR CAREER PATH

When you're picking a major, you're not just deciding what classes to fill your schedule with—you're also shaping your future career path, whether you realize it or not. Let's talk about how the major you choose can influence your career trajectory, the power of transferable skills, navigating grad school options, and what happens if you decide to switch majors.

Let's start with understanding career trajectories. It's pretty straightforward that a major in Education can lead you to teaching, or a degree in Computer Science can set you up in tech firms. But the paths can be less obvious too. For instance, a major in Philosophy doesn't just prepare you for pondering the meaning of life; it can also be a great launchpad into law, journalism, or any field that values critical thinking and clear communication. Or consider a major in Anthropology—beyond the obvious route of becoming an anthropologist, this degree is excellent for roles in international relations, public health, or urban planning, where insights into human behavior and cultural dynamics are invaluable.

One of the most valuable tools in any career field are often the transferable skills—those nifty abilities that are useful, no matter where you end up working. Skills like writing effectively, analyzing data, or managing projects are needed in just about any field. A major in History might seem locked into academia, but the research skills it hones are perfect for roles in research, policy making, or even marketing analytics. Similarly, a Drama major develops skills in presentation and creative thinking that are a boon in sales, event management, or education. So, when you're choosing your major, think beyond the content; consider the skills you'll be building and how they can apply across different sectors.

Your undergrad major can be a stepping stone to advanced studies, and sometimes, it's a requirement. If you're eyeing a future in medicine or a field like Physical Therapy, a Bachelor's is essential. Here's where it gets interesting—many graduate programs value a diverse academic background. Physical Therapy programs, for instance, appreciate candidates with degrees in anything from Biology to Kinesiology to Psychology, valuing the unique perspectives they bring. As long as all prerequisite courses are complete, graduate schools may look at applicants from a number of majors. So, if grad school is on your horizon, think about how your undergrad major can set you up for success, whether it's by meeting prerequisites or by giving you a unique edge.

What if halfway through, you realize that your chosen major isn't the love of your academic life? About 80% of college students change their major at least once during their college career. If you're contemplating this, it's crucial to consider the timing. Earlier is generally easier, as many courses can still count as electives or general education requirements. Talk to your advisor sooner rather than later to minimize any impact on your graduation timeline. And remember, changing your major isn't a sign of failure; it's an adaptation to your evolving interests and goals.

Wrapping up, your major can significantly influence your career path, but it's not a sole determinant. It's about the skills you develop, the passion you bring, and how you leverage your academic experiences into career opportunities. Whether you stick with your first choice or switch lanes, the journey is all about finding what works best for you and your future aspirations. Up next, we dive into internships and real-world experiences—because there's no substitute for testing the waters in actual professional settings.

BUILDING A PROFESSIONAL RESUME AND LINKEDIN PROFILE

In today's digital world, your online presence can be just as important as your real-world presence. If you're not on LinkedIn yet, now's the time to set up your profile. Think of your LinkedIn profile as your digital billboard. It's where you can showcase your skills, experiences, and professional accomplishments. Include a professional photo (not a blurry selfie), craft a compelling summary, and start connecting with classmates, professors, and professionals in your field.

Your resume and LinkedIn profile are fluid documents. Keep them updated as you gain new experiences and skills. Just scored an awesome internship? Add it. Took a leadership role in a club? That goes on there too. These tools are not just about listing your experiences; they're about telling your professional story. They're how you make your mark in the professional world, so make sure they reflect your best self.

CONNECTING WITH ALUMNI

First off, remember that alumni were once in your shoes, juggling lectures, exams, and perhaps a questionable diet. This common ground is your initial connection. Most universities have platforms dedicated to alumni relations. Register and create a profile that showcases your academic interests, extracurricular involvements, and career aspirations.

Many alumni keep their LinkedIn profiles updated, which makes it easier to find and connect with those in your field of interest. When reaching out, personalize your message. Mention specific details that resonate with their career path or express genuine curiosity about their industry insights. It's like sending a friend request, but with a professional twist. Engaging in alumni groups and participating in discussions can also increase your visibility and show your enthusiasm for your professional development.

Networking isn't just about taking; it's about mutual benefit. Think about what you can bring to the table, even as a student. Perhaps you can share insights from recent industry-related coursework or discuss campus developments. This approach can turn a one-time conversation into an ongoing exchange, laying the foundation for a robust professional relationship.

16

REFLECTING ON YOUR FRESHMAN YEAR: LESSONS LEARNED

Take a moment and think back to the person who stepped onto campus at the start of the year. Chances are, that version of you was a little less sure-footed, a tad more apprehensive, and a lot greener around the edges. Reflecting on your personal and academic growth isn't just about tallying up your GPA or listing the clubs you joined. It's deeper. It's about acknowledging the moments you pushed beyond your comfort zone or the times you rallied after a rough exam. Maybe you learned that you're more resilient than you thought, discovered a passion for medieval poetry, or realized that, yes, you can function on less sleep than you ever deemed possible (though, not recommended).

Take these insights and stack them up like your favorite books on your desk. They're your personal collection of truths and milestones that will help guide your decisions in the coming years. Did you find yourself thriving in discussions about global politics? Maybe a major in international relations is calling your name. Did you stumble in calculus but find solace and success in creative writing? It's all valuable intel for crafting your academic journey ahead.

ADAPTING TO CHANGES

If college teaches you anything, it's that change is the only constant. Reflect on how you've navigated the shifts and swerves of your freshman year. Maybe you switched dorms, faced down the challenge of remote classes, or learned to live with a roommate who's as nocturnal as a bat. Each change was a stepping stone to becoming more adaptable.

This adaptability isn't just crucial for surviving college; it's a life skill that you'll carry into your career and beyond. The ability to pivot and persevere is what turns potential setbacks into steps forward. So, whether it's switching majors or tackling an unforeseen group project, remember that with every change, you're fine-tuning your ability to navigate the new and unknown.

FEEDBACK FROM PEERS AND PROFESSORS

Feedback is more than just a grade on a paper or a comment in a class discussion—it's gold dust for your growth. Throughout your freshman year, you've likely received all kinds of feedback, from formal reviews from professors to offhand comments from classmates. Reflecting on this feedback means more than just nodding and moving on; it's about actively integrating this advice to refine your skills and approaches.

Did a professor suggest you dive deeper in your research? Maybe it's time to explore more comprehensive study methods or seek out additional sources. Did a friend point out that you shine in group studies? Consider forming or joining more study groups to enhance your learning. Embrace this feedback with an open mind—it's like receiving cheat codes for the game of college.

DOCUMENTING ACHIEVEMENTS

Documenting your achievements throughout your freshman year creates a tangible record of what you've accomplished and learned. This isn't just about padding your resume; it's about building a narrative of your college journey that you can reflect on and draw from in the future.

Whether it's a project you aced, a challenging course you navigated, or an extracurricular role you rocked, keep track of these milestones. Use a digital journal, a physical scrapbook, or an app—whatever fits your style. Think of this as your personal highlight reel, reminding you of your capabilities and achievements when you face new challenges or opportunities. This record is a powerful tool in your arsenal, helping to propel you forward and upward as you continue your college adventure.

SETTING GOALS FOR SOPHOMORE YEAR AND BEYOND

Remember, setting academic goals isn't just about choosing the right classes; it's about setting targets for what you want to achieve in those classes. Aim to improve your grades in challenging subjects, or maintain high marks in the areas you excel. And don't forget to throw some academic networking into the mix—professors and fellow students can offer invaluable advice and insights that textbooks just can't match.

While you're busy buffing up your academic and career prospects, don't forget about your personal development. College is the perfect time to work on becoming the well-rounded, grounded person you want to be. Think about setting goals that enhance your soft skills—leadership, communication, time management. Maybe you would like to take on a leadership role in a club or start a new group related to your interests. These experiences teach you how to manage both projects and people, a handy skill, no matter where you end up.

Finally, let's talk about work-life balance. Setting goals to keep your studies, work commitments, and personal life in harmony is crucial. It's about acknowledging that while college can sometimes feel like a frantic juggle between assignments, social life, and self-care, you need strategies to keep all the balls in the air.

Consider setting realistic study schedules, making time for exercise, and ensuring you have downtime to unwind. Remember, burning the candle at both ends isn't a sustainable strategy. Prioritize tasks, use tools like planners or apps to keep you organized, and don't be afraid to say no if it means overloading your plate. This balance is key to not just surviving college, but thriving in it.

By setting thoughtful, well-rounded goals for your sophomore year and beyond, you're not just planning for your next exam or semester; you're planning for a successful, fulfilling future. So, grab your planner, a cup of your favorite caffeinated beverage, and start sketching out your goals. Your future self will thank you for it.

LEADERSHIP AND EXTRACURRICULAR INVOLVEMENT: ENHANCING YOUR COLLEGE EXPERIENCE

Whether it's leading a student organization, managing a campus event, or spearheading a community service project, each role offers a unique buffet of challenges and rewards. These positions test your ability to navigate teams, solve problems on the fly, and keep your cool when the seas get rough. And here's the kicker: the skills you hone here—communication, teamwork, problem-solving—are exactly what future employers are starving for. So, next time there's an opening for a club officer or a student council position, why not throw your hat in the ring? If you snag the role, great! If not, no sweat—every attempt teaches you something valuable.

Joining clubs and organizations does more than fill your evenings and weekends—it fills your life with opportunities for personal growth, networking, and yes, a bit of fun. Whether you're into robotics, debate, dance, or anything in between, these groups allow you to explore your passions in a structured yet thrilling way. They're also fantastic for building a diverse network of peers who share your interests and might just turn into lifelong friends or future business partners. Plus, let's be honest, spicing up your study routine with activities you love can be a real sanity-saver during those marathon library sessions.

Balancing these exciting opportunities with your academics might seem like trying to juggle flaming torches while riding a unicycle. It's definitely not easy, but hey, it's not impossible either. Start with good old-fashioned time management—plan your weeks, know your peak productive times, and don't forget to carve out moments for rest. It's about finding that sweet spot where your studies and extracurriculars complement rather than compete with each other. And remember, it's perfectly okay to dial back or say no when things get too overwhelming. College is a marathon, not a sprint; keeping a steady pace will actually get you across the finish line in better shape.

Documenting these experiences is like keeping a treasure map of your college adventures. Each leadership role, each project, each event you organize adds a golden coin to your chest of accomplishments. Maintaining a detailed record (think digital portfolios or a well-groomed LinkedIn profile) helps you track your growth over time and showcases your achievements to potential employers or graduate schools. This isn't just about listing what clubs you were part of; it's about highlighting what you did, what skills you developed, and what impact you made. So, whether you organized the biggest campus fundraiser of the year or led your sports team to victory, make sure it's documented. When the time comes to set sail into the job market, this treasure trove of experiences might just be what sets you apart from the crowd.

In essence, diving into leadership roles and extracurricular activities during your college years is about more than just padding your resume—it's about crafting a college experience that's rich in growth, learning, and fun. It's about building the skills that textbooks can't teach and making memories that last a lifetime. So go ahead, take the helm, join the club, make your mark, and most importantly, enjoy the voyage. After all, this is your adventure—make it epic!

CONTINUING WELLNESS PRACTICES

Let's be honest, maintaining a wellness routine amidst the whirlwind of college life is akin to trying to keep a plant alive in a dorm room—it requires attention and consistency, but it's totally doable and definitely rewarding. Think back to those wellness habits you somehow managed to establish during your freshman year. Whether it was hitting the gym, choosing salad over fries (at least occasionally), or getting enough sleep to avoid resembling a zombie during 8 AM classes, these practices have been your lifelines.

Keeping these routines rolling isn't just about physical health; it's about setting the tone for your day-to-day energy and mental clarity. Regular exercise, for instance, isn't just about building muscles or stamina; it's about clearing the mental fog and boosting your mood. It's like hitting a reset button on your brain. And when it comes to food, think of your meals as fuel—what you put in is what you get out. A balanced diet can be your secret weapon against the mid-semester slump. Lastly, never underestimate the power of a good night's sleep. It's the best productivity hack any student can master—like giving your brain a nightly tune-up.

So, as you steam ahead into your next semesters, pencil in those gym sessions, stack your plate with veggies (yeah, pizza can be a veggie if you try hard enough), and hit the sack at a decent hour. Keeping these wellness routines is not about restricting your college experience; it's about enhancing it, ensuring you're always at your best, both physically and mentally.

MENTAL HEALTH MAINTENANCE

If college were a sea, mental health would be the undercurrent that can either smoothly sail you along or pull you under. Staying afloat means more than just the occasional feel-good activities; it involves consistent practices and sometimes, seeking lifelines. Mindfulness and meditation can be your anchors, helping you stay present and grounded amid the chaos of term papers and finals. Apps like Headspace offer guided sessions that fit perfectly into your packed schedule, providing a quick mental breather.

But sometimes, the stress gets too heavy, right? It's okay to admit when you're struggling. In fact, it's more than okay— it's important. Reaching out to campus counseling services isn't a sign of weakness; it's an action of strength. It's about taking charge of your well-being and ensuring you have the support to tackle whatever college throws your way. Also, keep the dialogue about mental health open with friends. Chances are, they're facing similar battles and sharing your experiences can provide mutual support and strengthen your bonds.

BALANCING SOCIAL LIFE

Speaking of friends, let's talk social life. It's the spice of college life, making every heavy study session or dreary lecture worth enduring. But like any spice, too much can be overwhelming, and too little, well, it's just bland. Striking that perfect balance between hitting the books and hitting the town involves some serious strategy—like planning your week ahead, squeezing in social time without overlapping major deadlines, and knowing when to say yes and when to take a rain check.

Remember, socializing isn't just about parties and hangouts; it's about building a community that uplifts and supports you. It's the coffee runs, the study groups, the late-night chats about everything and nothing—all these weave together to form your unique college experience, providing a network of support and a lot of good memories.

LIFE-LONG LEARNING AND GROWTH

Lastly, let's zoom out a bit and talk about the big picture—life-long learning. College is just one chapter in your education story, and the plot-line involves constant development and growth. Embrace every opportunity to learn, not just from textbooks and lectures, but from every experience and every person you meet. Whether it's picking up a new hobby, learning a new language, or tackling a subject outside your major, keep that curiosity alive.

And remember, personal development doesn't end with graduation. The skills, habits, and insights you gain during your college years are tools you'll carry throughout your life. They'll help you adapt to post-college challenges, whether in your career, your personal life, or your continued education. So keep feeding that brain of yours, keep challenging yourself, and most importantly, enjoy every learning moment.

As you turn the page from this chapter to the next, carry forward these wellness and self-care strategies. They're not just your survival kit for college but your toolkit for life, ensuring you keep growing, learning, and enjoying every step of the journey. Up next, we'll dive into how to wrap up your college experience with a bang, making sure you leave as a well-rounded, ready-to-tackle-the-world graduate. Stay tuned, the best is yet to come!

CONCLUSION

We've navigated through a maze of new beginnings, from setting up your dorm to figuring out where the least crowded study spots are. We've tackled building supportive relationships—shout out to that one roommate who just gets your weird snack cravings—and mastered the fine art of juggling classes with a somewhat respectable sleep schedule. Remember all those study skills we talked about? Yeah, those are going to keep paying off, trust me. And let's not forget the networking hustle and keeping your body and mind in check while keeping your bank account from diving into the red.

The key takeaways? Embrace your newfound independence, build that resilience muscle, and never stop growing—personally, academically, spiritually, you name it. Self-care isn't selfish; it keeps you running. Stress? Manage it like a pro. Balance is not just a word; it's your new best friend.

So, take a moment. Yes, right now. Reflect on your own journey that got you where you are today. Pat yourself on the back for the mountains climbed and the hurdles crossed. Each challenge you faced and lesson learned was a stepping stone to where you are right now.

Now, looking ahead, I want you to take all these strategies, insights, and good vibes and roll them into your sophomore year—and beyond. Create a personal action plan. Get involved. Find mentors. Keep building that support network. There's so much more to learn, explore, and discover.

And remember, you're not alone in this. Every college student faces ups and downs—it's a universal gig. But with a bit of grit, a dash of flexibility, and maybe a few more coffee runs, you'll navigate through beautifully.

I want to leave you with a little message from me:

I believe in you. I believe in your potential to not just survive, but to thrive. Approach the coming years with curiosity, enthusiasm, and an open heart. The world is full of opportunities, my friend— seize them and craft your own remarkable journey!

Keep pushing, keep dreaming, and above all, keep being the incredible person you are. Here's to more laughs, more learning, and an unforgettable college journey.

I wish you all the best,

Dr. Alvarez

Made in the USA
Columbia, SC
13 November 2024

46439147R00076